Guide to the First Article V Convention of the People

Guide to the First Article V Convention of the People

THE CONSTITUTIONAL PATH TO TAKING OUR COUNTRY BACK

Daniel J. Tekunoff

ISBN-13: 9781546598046
ISBN-10: 1546598049
Library of Congress Control Number: 2017908625
CreateSpace Independent Publishing Platform
North Charleston, South Carolina

Table of Contents

For My American People

Preface

I wrote Guide to the First Article V Convention of the People as a type of modern day Federalist Paper, in favor of our nation calling for an Article V convention for proposing constitutional amendments to the U.S. Constitution.

I wrote this book as a resource for all. It is an introduction and primer for legislators, scholars, judges, attorneys, and students of law and history to the problems surrounding the Article V Convention Clause in the U.S. Constitution. I also wrote this book in plain English, for the common person in America, to educate the public in relatively short order of the American People's right to modify their own government, and how best to preserve and promote our shared liberty through an Article V Convention of the People.

This Guide challenges and corrects the mistaken position of the Convention of the States movement. Such movement incorrectly asserts that state legislatures may take from the People our fundamental right to specially elect our representatives to any future constitutional convention. (See Chapter 9.) This book acts as a true guide for state legislators regarding how to handle an Article V convention.

Finally, this Guide gives direction to the California State Legislature, whose citizens through Proposition 59 on November 8, 2016 directed California's elected officials to use all of their Constitutional authority to overturn the U.S. Supreme Court case of Citizens United v. Federal Election Commission. The Citizens United case overturned a century of law and essentially allows unlimited spending in elections, which has the effect of cementing class division and wealth inequality.

There is only one thing which the California State Legislature can do to properly comply with Proposition 59 – vote for a General Convention for proposing constitutional amendments to the U.S. Constitution, pursuant to Article V. Article V does not provide for special interest constitutional conventions. Such conventions are meant to involve the entire nation, with all having an opportunity to be heard. Only a General Convention, with full powers to propose such amendments as it determines is best suited to correct errors and improve the Constitution, may be called per Article V and the terms of the U.S. Constitution.

It is time for state legislatures to put aside the constitutionally unauthorized practice of requesting limited topic or single subject conventions. To lead the country toward its first Article V Convention of the People, state legislators should instead push for a vote in favor of an unlimited General Convention for proposing constitutional amendments, pursuant to Article V of the U.S. Constitution.

INTRODUCTION

Why We Study the Article V Convention Clause

"The people are the King."[1]

(GOUVERNEUR MORRIS, U.S. CONSTITUTIONAL
CONVENTION, JULY 20, 1787)

THE PEOPLE ARE THE KING. That was the innovation of the United States Constitution written in 1787. Instead of the American political system assuming that our sovereign is the King or the government itself, our system assumes that **the People are the sovereign** and that the government may only wield those powers which the People have delegated to it.[2] Republican constitutions are "derived from the people with no intermediaries, so that sovereignty in practice reside[s] in the people."[3]

Who holds original power in our system? How does one structure a constitution so that the People truly hold original power? What clause in the U.S. Constitution protects the People's shared original power to make and alter their own government? The Framers of the U.S. Constitution were wise. They foresaw that a day would come when our system would become out of balance, what people today call broken government. To protect the original power of the People to make modifications to government, the Framers kept open a direct path for the People to amend government. The second alternative in the amending article, Article V, provides for a Convention of the People for the purpose of proposing constitutional amendments.

One of our most precious freedoms is the freedom to change our own form of government. George Washington, in his Farewell Address, stated that "[t]he basis of our political systems is **the right of the people to make and alter their constitutions of government**." If a people are not free to make changes to their own government, then the people are not free. The People's collective right and power to make and to alter their own form of government is considered an essential element of a free, representative republic. The freedom to change our own form of government was intended to be protected by the Article V Convention Clause. Article V (roman numeral 5) of the U.S. Constitution allows the U.S. Congress to initiate the process of proposing constitutional amendments, but leaves open a path to the People, through a constitutional convention, to amend the Constitution as well.

All Americans must be aware of our right to change our own Constitution through an Article V convention. The Article V convention is the People's peaceful check and balance when government is no longer working properly. Once the national legislature has become corrupt, it cannot be relied upon to propose appropriate amendments. Per Article V, the state legislatures must be pressed to vote for the Call of the Convention. In our system, it is the People themselves who are expected to ensure that state legislators preserve the People's peaceful path to altering our own Constitution. In the more formal style of the time, James Madison, in The Federalist No. 51, described our **check and balance system**[4] as follows:

> "This policy of supplying, by opposite and rival interests, the defect of better motives, might be traced through the whole system of human affairs, private as well as public. We see it particularly displayed in all the subordinate distributions of power, where the constant aim is to divide and arrange the several offices in such a manner as that each may be a check on the other – **that the private interest of every individual may be a sentinel over the public rights**."[5]

Our shared right to a Convention of the People is only one of the essential elements of free government,[6] but **without it we do not have full protection for the other fundamental principles of a representative republic.**

Full representation is another essential element of a representative government. As you will learn in Chapter 2, our nation now has partial, or rationed representation, due to a failure to make sure there are enough representatives to support full representation for a nation of 325 million inhabitants. Of all the principles of a free people, full representation must be most carefully guarded. We consent to being governed by representatives in exchange for full and actual representation. Without full representation, we do not have the voluntary consent necessary to qualify as a nation of free people.

Another fundamental principle of a representative republic is the principle of **fair, free, full and frequent elections**. "The elective mode of obtaining rulers is the characteristic policy of republican government."[7] Frequent elections allow the People to periodically remove representatives who do not perform, and guard against the legislature using the military against the People[8]. Full elections mean that all citizens have a right to vote, and for the elections to constitute a free and fair system, all citizens must have an equal vote (known as a one person, one vote system.) Free people agree that their votes will be equal. In The Federalist No. 52, James Madison wrote:

> **"The definition of the right of suffrage is very justly regarded as a fundamental article of republican government.** It was incumbent on the Convention therefore to define and establish this right, in the Constitution."[9]

While the delegates to the 1787 Constitutional Convention spent much of their four months discussing and defining the voting rules for our new government, they spent no time discussing the rules of suffrage for the Article V Convention. Intentionally or not, they left the task to us. It is now the responsibility of the People to be sentinels over the process and ensure that the voting rules for an Article V convention are consistent with rule by the People.

Another essential element of a republican constitution is **a system of checks and balances** and the adoption of **the Doctrine of Separation of Powers**[10] (to be distinguished from the Doctrine of Unity of Powers utilized in a socialist constitution[11].) When the system of checks and balances breaks down for lack of maintenance (maintenance coming by way of an Article V Convention to propose constitutional amendments,) the branches cross over check and balance lines and the People experience this as abusive government. As George Washington stated in his Farewell Address:

> "It is **important**, likewise, that the habits of thinking in a free country should inspire caution in those entrusted with its administration to **confine themselves within their respective constitutional spheres, avoiding in the exercise of the powers of one department to encroach upon another. The spirit of encroachment tends to consolidate the powers of all the departments in one and thus to create, whatever the form of government, a real despotism.** A just estimate of that love of power and proneness to abuse it which predominates in the human heart is sufficient to satisfy us of the truth of this position."[12]

A republican form of government best suits popular sovereignty because it allows a separation of powers and a check and balance system. If we all treated each other as free people, these would be among the Constitutional rules that we would choose.

Another fundamental principle of a representative republic is that it is **limited by the Rule of Law**, rather than rule by men.[13] Related concepts are that **all persons are equal under the law,** and that the **laws will be applied consistently.**[14] A **Bill of Rights** helps to both establish and support the Rule of Law. It is the People's belief in a system of free government and veneration for the Rule of Law which gives us stability and the opportunity to work toward a satisfying life. When respect for the Rule of Law breaks down in society, it is a sign that the system is not working properly and the remedy provided under the U.S. Constitution is a Convention of the People for proposing constitutional amendments per Article V.

A basic principle of a free republic is that of **virtue in representation**[15]. Through elections, it is theorized that the People will choose representatives that set their personal interests aside and are able to work for the common good.[16] In The Federalist No. 57, Madison stated:

> "The aim of every political constitution is, or ought to be, first to obtain for rulers men who possess most wisdom to discern, and most virtue to pursue, the common good of the society; and in the next place, to take the most effectual precautions for keeping them virtuous whilst they continue to hold the public trust."[17]

When the citizens lose faith in the virtue and wisdom of their national representatives, one remedy is for our state representatives to push for an Article V Convention of the People.

Related to the concept of virtue is the concept of **energy or vigor** in the system. If a representative republic is healthy, there will be energy and vigor in the system which is the force that does the People's necessary work.[18] When congresspersons use a "no compromise" philosophy as a rule rather than an exception, it robs the governing system of its energy. The end result of such behavior may not be felt by congresspersons and their millionaire families. However, when the system is not working properly due to lack of compromise and virtue in our so-called representatives, the suffering is experienced most by those without material wealth. Extended periods of "enlightened statesmen" not being "at the helm" results in the populace losing respect for the Rule of Law and threatens the system itself.

Another way to look at a republican form of government is to understand that it tries to **prevent hereditary systems of government and dictatorships** of all types. When we see signs of the same families dominating positions of power or of an executive branch which simply ignores check and balance limitations, it is time for the state legislatures to call for an Article V convention to correct errors in the system allowing the destruction of free government.

Many of the problems we as a nation are seeing today are symptoms of a **decaying foundation of our republican principles**. Gerrymandering of the electoral districts is counter-democratic, as is an electoral system which has no effective rules or spending limits to ensure full participation in the governing process. Growing inequality of all sorts is a sign that the system is out of balance. Failure of the most privileged in society to make sure there are enough tax dollars in the system to properly educate the citizens in their basic civic duties and to keep enough police officers on the street reflects a loss of virtue in both government and business "leadership." All three branches of the national government now routinely exceed check and balance limits.

The U.S. Constitution gives us a remedy for these ills, a constitutional convention pursuant to Article V. The Article V Convention Clause intentionally funnels the nation into one peaceful process. This gives us the additional benefit of the possibility of a constitutional convention uniting the nation at a time when we need unity the most. James Madison, when urging the First House of Representatives to begin the work on a Bill of Rights on June 8, 1789, stated:

> "It appears to me that this house is bound by every motive of **prudence,** not to let the first session pass over without proposing to the state legislatures **some things to be incorporated into the constitution, as will render it as acceptable to the whole people of the United States, as it has been found acceptable to a majority of them.**"[19]

One of the purposes of the Article V convention is to give us, as a nation, **a way to bind together and unite** once again. The Article V convention allows us to find the best of our nation to represent us, and to re-commit to our shared sovereignty. It is our nation's one and only peaceful path when Congress becomes corrupt or incompetent. The Framers had the wisdom to provide the People with a peaceful path to modify our government through an Article V convention. What happened to our wisdom, that we do not take the Article V route built for times like this?

Because Article V is our only peaceful path to constitutional amendment when Congress will not act, we must continue to study it and demand that our state legislators vote for an Article V convention when Congress becomes corrupt or any of the branches of national government cross check and balance boundaries.[20] The slow erosion of the foundational principles of a representative republic has resulted in various non-democratic and counter-democratic processes, such as gerrymandering, wealth dominance in the governing process, primary elections designed to favor candidates pre-chosen by wealthy groups of individuals, and economic, education, and criminal justice systems defined by their inequalities and injustice. Calling an Article V convention and returning our system to compliance with fundamental principles of a free republic should, over time, reverse the unhealthy and unequal trends in our various systems.

About ten years before the Declaration of Independence, American leaders took up the call to the American people to start studying the nature of government and those principles that make a representative republic.[21] It is now time for Americans to once again study the principles of a free, representative republic.

For those of us who have taken an oath to support the U.S. Constitution[22], studying the Article V Convention Clause is even more important. The oath provides a floor, criminal liability, but there is no ceiling to our oath other than each individual's capacity for hard work and sacrifice. Article V cannot support criminal liability under the oath because Article V is too vague for criminal liability to attach. Nonetheless, the oath provides a standard for discussions regarding what we are supposed to do as a nation when representative government does not represent all Americans.

If the oath means that one cannot advocate the violent overthrow of the government, then it would also mean working to keep open the peaceful path of a People's constitutional convention in order to help stave off any attempts at violent overthrow. Article IV, Section 4 of the Constitution guarantees a republican form of government. When we take an oath to "support" the U.S. Constitution, it means we are making a lifetime vow to support the fundamental principles of a representative republic because these are the principles that promote our collective freedom.

Those who are not vigilant of their rights lose them. The Article V Convention Clause has never been used. Is it now time? Read on and decide.

CHAPTER 1

The Two Primary Structural Defects in the United States Constitution

"Experience must be our only guide. Reason may mislead us."

(JOHN DICKINSON, DELEGATE FROM DELAWARE, AT
U.S. CONSTITUTIONAL CONVENTION, AUGUST 13, 1787)

WE OFTEN HEAR COMMENTS LIKE "Why would you want to mess with the U.S. Constitution?" Ordinarily, you would not. "Conventions are serious things, and ought not to be repeated," declared Charles Pinckney on the second to last day of the 1787 U.S. Constitutional Convention.[1] Blessedly, the Framers of the U.S. Constitution were not so arrogant to think that their work would last without need of amendment from time to time. This is why an amendment clause was placed into the U.S. Constitution, at Article V.

There are two pathways in Article V to amend the U.S. Constitution. The first pathway is through the U.S. Congress. When Congress will not act, there is only one pathway – a convention to propose amendments to the Constitution, when two-thirds of the states' legislatures vote for the call of the convention.[2]

Article V was written at the Constitutional Convention of 1787, in Philadelphia (which took place May 25 to September 17, 1787.) **We have never utilized the convention path of Article V. It is an untested proceeding.**

After the Constitution was written, demands were made for a Bill of Rights. The Bill of Rights was written by the First Congress in 1789.

James Madison proposed draft amendments at the First Congress on June 8, 1789.[3] Congress worked on the proposed Bill of Rights between July 21, 1789 and September 25, 1789.[4]

Between the completion of the original Constitution and the Bill of Rights, the Framers generally categorized possible amendments into two categories: 1) structural amendments ("changes in the structure and powers of the new federal government[5],"); and 2) individual and minority rights related amendments, designed to "protect personal liberties."[6] The supporters of the Constitution were willing to support rights related amendments in order to gain the support necessary to approve the new Constitution, but wanted to avoid changes to the check and balance structure until experience teaches us where structural defects are located.[7]

The quote at the beginning of this chapter, by John Dickinson, states a recurring theme in relation to making modifications to our founding document. Prior to the First Congress' work on the Bill of Rights, George Washington gave his inaugural address on April 30, 1789. Washington provided the following wisdom regarding when to amend the U.S. Constitution:

"Besides the ordinary objects submitted to your care, it will remain with your judgment to decide, how far an exercise of the occasional power delegated by the Fifth article of the Constitution is rendered expedient at the present juncture by the nature of objections which have been urged against the System, or by the degree of inquietude which has given birth to them . . . For I assure myself that whilst you carefully avoid every alteration which might endanger the benefits of an United and effective Government, or which ought to await the future lessons of experience; a reverence for the characteristic rights of freemen, and a regard for the public harmony, will sufficiently influence your deliberations on the question how far the former can be more impregnably fortified, or the latter be safely and advantageously promoted."[8]

Illustration 1:

THE DEVIL'S LOOP OF THE AMERICAN CONSTITUTION

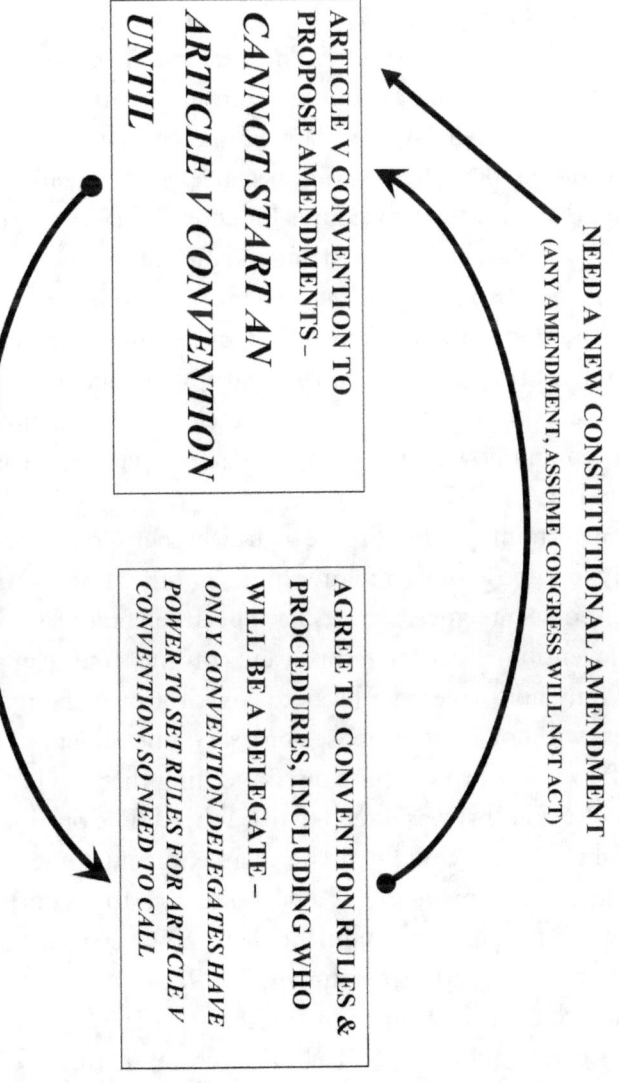

NEED A NEW CONSTITUTIONAL AMENDMENT
(ANY AMENDMENT, ASSUME CONGRESS WILL NOT ACT)

ARTICLE V CONVENTION TO
PROPOSE AMENDMENTS –
*CANNOT START AN
ARTICLE V CONVENTION
UNTIL*

AGREE TO CONVENTION RULES &
PROCEDURES, INCLUDING WHO
WILL BE A DELEGATE –
*ONLY CONVENTION DELEGATES HAVE
POWER TO SET RULES FOR ARTICLE V
CONVENTION, SO NEED TO CALL*

Over 230 years have passed since the U.S. Constitution was written. In that time, the lessons of experience have taught us that there are two primary <u>structural</u> defects in the United States Constitution.

One error is in the Convention Clause contained within Article V, the amendment article of our Constitution. The defect is that the rules and procedures to start any U. S. constitutional convention are not set forth within the Constitution itself. While many of the rules and procedures can be developed by the delegates sitting in convention, much as in the 1787 Convention[9], the rules and procedures for choosing delegates cannot be developed until there are delegates sitting in convention.

Illustration 1, *The Devil's Loop of the American Constitution* (see page 3,) demonstrates the defect in the Article V Convention Clause. Before we can have a constitutional convention **for any purpose,** some agreement must be made as to a number of issues, including how convention delegates are chosen and how many voting delegates each state may send to the convention.

Due to this uncertainty and a dispute as to whether Congress or the state legislatures can impose subject matter limits or other limits on a constitutional convention, state governments have been reluctant to call for a constitutional convention. This dangerously cuts off the American people from using their only non-violent pathway to constitutional change when the U.S. Congress will not act to propose necessary amendments.

The second flaw is a defect of omission, something that was left out of the original Constitution that was intended to be there. The original **proposed** Bill of Rights of 1789 contained twelve amendments, not ten, and each proposed amendment was there for a purpose. As it turns out, eleven of the original twelve proposed amendments have now been ratified, the eleventh as our Twenty-Seventh Amendment in 1992.

The one proposed original amendment that was never ratified by enough states was <u>originally intended</u> to limit each representative in the House of Representatives to representing no more than 50,000 American citizens. Making sure there are enough members in our House of Representatives is considered an essential element of a republican form of government.[10] James Madison, considered the father of our Constitution, in The Federalist Number 39, stated:

> It is *essential* to such a government, that it be derived from the great body of society, not from an inconsiderable portion, or a favored class of it; otherwise a handful of tyrannical nobles, exercising their oppressions by a delegation of their powers, might aspire to the rank of republicans, and claim for their government the honorable title of republic.[11]

The original intent of the Size of Congress Amendment was frustrated at the last minute in conference committee without any record of why. The proposal is confusingly written, and looked ahead only thirty years. Such proposal was one vote away from becoming part of the Constitution, but the drafting problems and the addition of Vermont as the fourteenth state stunted the momentum of the passage of the amendment. The original proposed first amendment, its drafting problems, and its essential necessity in a republic have been forgotten for almost 230 years.

This book examines these two constitutional defects, with reference to the actual records of the Constitutional Convention of 1787 and the actual records of the First Congress in 1789, when the Bill of Rights was written. The book is designed to give you the power of knowledge, as you do not need to trust the word of politicians or lawyers. You will be able to confirm public claims about the Constitution by checking the record yourself, often for free because The Records of the Federal Convention of 1787 (a three-volume set edited by Max Farrand and published in 1911) are out of copyright, part of the public domain and readily available for download over the internet. The Federalist Papers, 85 articles written by James Madison, Alexander Hamilton and John Jay to explain the new Constitution and convince the American people to ratify it, are also available for free over the internet.

Most importantly, however, is **the solution** I have developed to address both problems. We are literally able to update and upgrade our

United States Constitution to address both structural defects with one structural change, like shooting two apples with one arrow. The solution involves adding a third body to Congress, with check and balance powers. We will split Congress not into two divisions, but three divisions, going from a bicameral legislature to a tricameral legislature. The constitutional amendment to effectuate this change I call **The Tricameralism Amendment.**

CHAPTER 2

The Story of the Bill of Rights and the First Twelve Amendments

*"That useful alterations will be suggested by experience, could not but be foreseen. It was requisite, therefore, that a mode for introducing them should be provided. The mode preferred by the convention seems to be stamped with every mark of propriety. It guards equally against that extreme facility, which would render the Constitution too mutable; and **that extreme difficulty, which might perpetuate its discovered faults.**"*[1]

(James Madison, The Federalist No. 43, January 23, 1788)

I start by telling The Story of The Bill of Rights and The First Twelve Amendments to The United States Constitution. "Wait," you might say, "the Bill of Rights are the first ten amendments to the Constitution." That is correct, but what most Americans do not know is that in Congress' First Session, in 1789, Congress sent to the states **twelve** amendments as the proposed Bill of Rights.[2] The Founding Fathers intended to have not ten but <u>twelve amendments</u> in The Bill of Rights, as part of an overall structure of checks and balances (See Appendix 1: *The Documentary Record of the Bill of Rights' Passage Through the First Congress of the United States of America.*) The Bill of Rights we know and love today are the ten amendments ratified by three quarters of the early state legislatures.

Table 1
State Ratifications of United States Constitution
(proposed September 17, 1787)

1.	Delaware	December 7, 1787
2.	Pennsylvania	December 12, 1787
3.	New Jersey	December 18, 1787
4.	Georgia	January 2, 1788
5.	Connecticut	January 9, 1788
6.	Massachusetts	February 6, 1788
7.	Maryland	April 26, 1788
8.	South Carolina	May 23, 1788
9.	New Hampshire	June 21, 1788
10.	Virginia	June 25, 1788
11.	New York	July 26, 1788
12.	North Carolina	November 21, 1789
13.	Rhode Island	May 29, 1790

Table 2
State Ratifications of Bill of Rights
(proposed September 25, 1789)

1.	New Jersey	November 20, 1789
2.	Maryland	December 19, 1789
3.	North Carolina	December 22, 1789
4.	South Carolina	January 19, 1790
5.	New Hampshire	January 25, 1790
6.	Delaware	January 28, 1790
7.	New York	February 27, 1790
8.	Pennsylvania	March 10, 1790
9.	Rhode Island	June 7, 1790
10.	Vermont*	November 3, 1791
11.	Virginia	December 15, 1791

* Vermont joined the United States of America, as the fourteenth state, on March 4, 1791. This caused the ¾ requirement of the Article V ratification clause to increase from 10 of 13 states to 11 of 14 states.

July 4, 1776 is the date the thirteen American colonies declared independence from Great Britain. The United States Constitution was written at the Constitutional Convention of 1787. The United States of America was not formed as one nation under the United States Constitution until it was ratified by the ninth state, New Hampshire, on June 21, 1788.[3] (See Table 1: *State Ratifications of United States Constitution*.) In 1789, George Washington began his first term as President and the First Congress of the United States prepared the proposed Bill of Rights as amendments to the Constitution.

At the Constitutional Convention of 1787, before the delegates had completed their work, there was already talk of holding a second constitutional convention.[4] After the text of the original Constitution was published, adding amendments to the Constitution became the primary issue in the federal elections of 1789.[5] Concerned about a second constitutional convention destroying the work of the first, James Madison decided to throw his weight behind adding a Bill of Rights to cut off the movement for a second convention.[6]

As a member of the House of Representatives in the First Congress of the United States of America, Madison pushed the House to take up, prepare and propose a Bill of Rights. The House began its work on June 8, 1789, and a proposed Bill of Rights with **twelve amendments** was approved by Congress on September 25, 1789 and signed on September 28, 1789.[7] Today's Bill of Rights with ten amendments became part of the U.S. Constitution on December 15, 1791, when Virginia was the eleventh state to ratify our Bill of Rights.[8] (See Table 2: *State Ratifications of Bill of Rights*.)

This chapter tells the story of the two amendments of the proposed first twelve that were not originally ratified by three quarters of the state legislatures.

A. THE CONGRESSIONAL PAY AMENDMENT

Many people are surprised to learn that we have actually ratified eleven of the first twelve proposed constitutional amendments. What is today's

Twenty-Seventh Amendment (the last amendment to become part of the U.S. Constitution) was one of the first twelve, ratified in 1992, over two-hundred years after its proposal in 1789.[9] It was ratified by the thirty-eighth state on May 7, 1992.[10] My suspicion is that most adults of the time have no memory of the passage of the Twenty-Seventh Amendment because the Los Angeles Riots of 1992 started on April 29, 1992, and concerns for public safety diverted attention away from any news of a 203 year old constitutional amendment proposal finally getting ratified.[11]

The Congressional Pay Amendment (sometimes referred to in the scholarly literature as the "compensation amendment"[12]) was one of the two proposed amendments that did not make the "original cut" into The Bill of Rights. The originally intended second amendment, now our Twenty-Seventh Amendment, states:

> "No law, varying the compensation for the services of the Senators and Representatives, shall take effect, until an election of Representatives shall have intervened."[13]

The Constitution, unfortunately, places Congress in a conflict of interest by giving Congresspersons the right to set their own pay. (See U.S. Constitution, Article I, Section 6, paragraph 1.) The intent behind the Congressional Pay Amendment is to slow Congress down in giving itself pay raises. It prevents the possibility of Congress giving itself retroactive pay raises, and forces Congress to wait until after the next election to get any raise which Congress may have voted for itself. This theoretically gives people a chance to vote in a new Representative (but not necessarily a new Senator) upon competing candidates' promises to reverse the raise.

In terms of checks and balances, the Twenty-Seventh Amendment is a relatively weak force against congressional corruption. A better option would be to remove the conflict of interest altogether, and place the decision on how much Senators and Representatives get paid in the hands of a body other than the Senators and Representatives themselves.

Table 3: *Congressional Pay History*[1]

Between March 4, 1789 and March 3, 1817, U.S. Congressmen were generally paid six dollars per diem.[2] From March 3, 1817 to December 3, 1855, congressional pay was increased to eight dollars per diem.[3] In 1855, Congress succeeded in switching to an annual salary. The historical per annum salaries for members of Congress are as follows:

Historical per Annum Salaries for Members of Congress

December 3, 1855	$3,000	January 1, 1985	$75,100
December 4, 1865	$5,000	January 1, 1987	$77,400
March 4, 1871	$7,500	February 4, 1987	$89,500
January 20, 1874	$5,000	February 1, 1990	$96,600 (Reps.)
March 4, 1907	$7,500		$98,400 (Senators)
March 4, 1925	$10,000	January 1, 1991	$125,100 (Reps.)
July 1, 1932	$ 9,000		$101,900 (Senators)
April 1, 1933	$ 8,500	August 14, 1991	$125,100 (Senators)
February 1, 1934	$ 9,000	January 1, 1992	$129,500
July 1, 1934	$ 9,500	January 1, 1993	$133,600
April 4, 1935	$10,000	January 1, 1998	$136,700
January 3, 1947	$12,500	January 1, 2000	$141,300
March 1, 1955	$22,500	January 1, 2001	$145,100
January 3, 1965	$30,000	January 1, 2002	$150,000
March 1, 1969	$42,500	January 1, 2003	$154,700
October 1, 1975	$44,600	January 1, 2004	$158,100
March 1, 1977	$57,500	January 1, 2005	$162,100
October 1, 1979	$60,662.50	January 1, 2006	$165,200
Dec. 18, 1982 (Reps.)/	$69,800	January 1, 2008	$169,300
July 1, 1983 (Senators)		January 1, 2009	$174,000
January 1, 1984	$72,600		

---

1. Ida A. Brudnick, *Salaries of Members of Congress: Recent Actions and Historical Tables*, Congressional Research Service, December 19, 2014, at pp. 10-13.

2. *Id.*, at p. 11.

3. *Ibid.*

Originally, six states ratified the Congressional Pay Amendment.[14] At the time, that was less than half of the original thirteen colonies, and you need, at Congress' option, three quarters of state legislatures or state ratification conventions to pass a constitutional amendment.[15]

Ohio, upset over Congress giving itself a retroactive pay raise known as the "Salary Grab Act", added its vote in 1873.[16] The Salary Grab Act raised Congress' pay from $5,000 per year to $7,500 per year, but made the raise retroactive to 1871, giving members of Congress an additional $5,000 bonus in income.[17]

Then, in the 1960's, we begin to see signs of disconnection and corruption working into our Constitutional system as Congress begins to give itself heftier and more frequent pay raises (See Table 3: *Congressional Pay History*, at page 11.) (Note: The use of the word "corruption" here does not necessarily relate to human corruption, but includes the possibility that the foundations of our check and balance system itself have not been maintained for such a long time that they are beginning to weaken and have become corroded or "corrupted" from lack of maintenance.)

Early in our Constitutional history, Congress was slow to raise its pay. In the Twentieth Century, senators and representatives in Congress transition from being "part-timers" to full time career politicians.[19] Over the 34 years from 1935 to 1969, Congress gave itself only three raises, going from a salary of $10,000 per year to a salary of $30,000 per year.

In just 22 years, from 1969 to 1991, Congress gave itself 14 raises, resulting in 1991 Congressional salaries of $125,100. The 1985 salary was $75,100, but in just six years Congress gave itself $50,000 worth of raises, to end up in 1991 with a salary of $125,100. It was a sign that the U.S. Congress was becoming less and less responsive to its own citizens. More ominously, however, it was a sign that the foundations of our constitutional system were weakening and that the citizenry could no longer count on Congress to take ordinary citizens' views into account.

In 1982, Gregory D. Watson, then a sophomore at the University of Texas, became aware of the unratified Congressional Pay Amendment and wondered if it was still alive and could be ratified.[20] He discovered that the proposed amendment had no internal time limit, wrote a paper with his analysis and urged that the amendment be adopted.[21] Mr. Watson's professor gave him a C for the paper he wrote, humbling his student with the comment that the proposed amendment was a "dead letter" and would never become part of the Constitution.[22]

Gregory D. Watson had the last laugh. He began a one-man campaign to get state legislatures to ratify the Congressional Pay Amendment.[23] Maine ratified in 1983.[24] Colorado ratified in 1984.[25] Watson discovered that Wyoming had ratified the amendment in 1978.[26] Thirty-one more state ratifications came in between 1985 and 1992.[27] In 1992, Michigan beat New Jersey to become the thirty-eighth state (the magic number to reach the three-quarter threshold under Article V) to ratify the Congressional Pay Amendment, and Illinois and California came in 40th and 41st for good measure.[28] Gregory D. Watson became one of those rare inspirational examples that just one person can still make a difference.

After having been an open proposal for 202 years, what could have been our first or second constitutional amendment is instead the most recent amendment, the Twenty-Seventh. We actually have eleven amendments in our Bill of Rights, if you were to view it from the perspective of the people who in 1789 wrote the proposed Bill of Rights with twelve amendments. More importantly for the purposes of constitutional modification, **the Twenty-Seventh Amendment was a lesson taught to us by time and experience that there was a structural defect in the Constitution that needed to be corrected.**

Unfortunately, while the Congressional Pay Amendment did slow Congress down from giving itself raises, it did not address the gradual corruption of our Constitutional system. The corruption is still there, and growing. All systems must be maintained, or they wear out their usefulness and break down.

Experience taught us that we should have ratified an early proposed amendment considered important to the check and balance structure of the U.S. Constitution. Now, we look at the one amendment proposed by the First Congress in 1789 that has still not made it into the Constitution in some form. If we missed ratifying one important amendment from the originally proposed twelve amendments, chances are the second one not ratified was also important and may be part of the reason the system no longer seems to be working properly.

B. The Size of Congress Amendment

Now we look at the last of the originally proposed twelve amendments, the one that came first on the original list. The first proposed amendment would have amended Article 1, section 2 of the U.S. Constitution, which has always required at least 30,000 people per representative. It is this missing first amendment which must be modernized and added to the U.S. Constitution in order to complete the Bill of Rights. Essentially, our nation missed a step right at the beginning of its formation, and over the course of over two centuries, the defect is becoming more and more apparent.

As stated near the beginning of this chapter, James Madison had made a decision to pursue a Bill of Rights in the First Congress, in order to defend against a push for a second constitutional convention. On July 21, 1789, the first House of Representatives voted to appoint a select committee, with one person from each state, to report a set of draft amendments.[29] The select committee worked quickly, and just one week later, on July 28, 1789, produced its committee report.[30] The Committee of the Whole House met from August 13 through August 18, and debated in detail the proposed amendments, clause by clause.[31] The House began formal debate on August 19, 1789, and approved 17 draft amendments on August 24, 1789.[32] The first on the list was The Size of Congress amendment, which would require one representative for every 30,000 to 50,000 Americans.[33]

The seventeen proposed amendments were sent from the House to the Senate. Between September 2 and September 9, 1789, the Senate paired down the amendments to twelve, and weakened some of them.[34] The Senate Committee retained the basic meaning of the proposed first amendment, changing it only by proposing that we have one representative for every 30,000 to 60,000 people.[35]

Before going to the conference committee (a committee of both House of Representatives and Senate members which works out differences in language between the House version and Senate version of legislation,) the language of the Senate and House versions of the original first amendment were in near agreement. The House version required one representative for every 30,000 to 50,000 people, while the Senate version expanded the requirement to one representative for every 30,000 to 60,000 people. With that simple difference, one would think that the final version coming out of conference committee might have required one representative for every 30,000 to 55,000 people, as a compromise. What came out of conference committee was something drastically different, and because the committee kept no record of its proceedings, we know little of what transpired during the conference committee to cause the change. The progression of the language is as follows:

HOUSE OF REPRESENTATIVES FIRST VERSION OF PROPOSED FIRST AMENDMENT, August 24, 1789

After the first enumeration, required by the first Article of the Constitution, there shall be one Representative for every thirty thousand until the number shall amount to one hundred after which the proportion shall be so regulated by Congress that there shall be not less than one hundred Representatives nor less than one Representative for every forty thousand persons, until the number of representatives shall amount to two hundred after which the proportion shall be so regulated by Congress, that there shall not be less than two hundred Representatives, <u>nor less than one Representative for every fifty thousand persons.</u>[36]

SENATE'S REVISED VERSION, September 9, 1789

After the first enumeration, required by the first article of the Constitution, there shall be one Representative for every thirty thousand, until the number shall amount to one hundred; to which number one Representative shall be added for every subsequent increase of forty thousand, until the Representatives shall amount to two hundred, to which number <u>one Representative shall be added for every subsequent increase of sixty thousand persons.</u>[37]

FINAL CONFERENCE COMMITTEE VERSION, September 25, 1789

After the first enumeration required by the first Article of the Constitution, there shall be one Representative for every thirty thousand, until the number shall amount to one hundred, after which, the proportion shall be so regulated by Congress, that there shall be not less than one hundred Representatives, nor less than one Representative for every forty thousand persons, until the number of Representatives shall amount to two hundred, after which the proportion shall be so regulated by Congress, that there shall not be less than two hundred Representatives, <u>nor more than one Representative for every fifty thousand persons.</u>[38]

The final version goes back to the more confusing early House language, but changes the last phrase from "<u>nor **less** than one Representative for every fifty thousand persons</u>" to "<u>nor **more** than one Representative for every fifty thousand persons.</u>"[39] The change is subtle, but completely changes the proposed requirement that an individual's voting power not be diluted so much that he or she effectively has no real vote. (See Appendix 2: *Evolution of Language of Original Proposed First Amendment Limiting How Many People Each Member of House of Representatives May Represent*.) From a modern perspective, there is no real difference between the Constitution's original language in Article I ("The Number of Representatives shall not exceed one for every thirty Thousand . . .") and the effect that the originally proposed Size of Congress Amendment would have had. The conference committee completely eliminated the requirement to add a representative for every growth of fifty-thousand to sixty-thousand people.

We still have at least 30,000 people per representative <u>and</u> at least 50,000 people per representative. In fact, we are approaching 750,000 people per representative, and that is not representation. In fact, with only 535 people in Congress (435 in the House of Representatives and 100 in the Senate) in a nation of over 320 million people, Congress does not even produce an accurate sampling of citizen opinion upon which to make their decisions for all of us. Representation has become so diluted that we are literally no longer a democracy or a republic.

The U.S. Constitution, however, guarantees a republican form of government.[40] A republican form of government requires citizens to give up the right to vote on proposed laws and give that power to a representative, but not to such an extent that the representative does not provide meaningful representation to his or her voters. If the so called "representative" does not provide meaningful and responsive representation, it is not a republican form of government. James Madison, in The Federalist Number 10, discussed a type of "Goldilocks Zone" for a republic:

> "In the first place, it is to be remarked that, however small the republic may be, <u>the representatives must be raised to a certain number, in order to guard against the cabals of a few</u>; and that, however large it may be, they must be limited to a certain number, in order to guard against the confusion of a multitude.

> It must be confessed that in this, as in most other cases, there is a mean, on both sides of which inconveniences will be found to lie. <u>By enlarging too much the number of electors [voters], you render the representatives too little acquainted with all their local circumstances and lesser interests</u>; as [sic] by reducing it too much, you render him unduly attached to these, and too little fit to comprehend and pursue great and national objects."[41]

Our legislative branch long ago left the definition of a republic. When the Constitution was ratified, the people of our nation expected that they would share a representative in Congress with around 30,000 people, the number set forth in Article I, Section 2, paragraph 3 of the Constitution.[42] In large part, this expectation was based upon the writings of James Madison, writing as Publius, in the Federalist Papers. Madison deals with the issue of the ratio of voters to each representative in the House of Representatives in The Federalist Numbers 55, 56 and 58.

The Federalist Number 55, in relevant part, states:

"THE NUMBER of which the House of Representatives is to consist, forms another and a very interesting point of view, under which this branch of the federal legislature may be contemplated . . .

. . . The charges exhibited against it are, **first**, that **so small a number of representatives will be an unsafe depositary of the public interests**; **secondly**, that they will not possess a proper knowledge of the local circumstances of their numerous constituents; **thirdly**, that they will be taken from that class of citizens which will sympathize least with the feelings of the mass of the people, and be most likely to aim at a permanent elevation of the few on the depression of the many; **fourthly**, **that defective as the number will be in the first instance, it will be more and more disproportionate, by the increase of the people, and the obstacles which will prevent a correspondent increase of the representatives**. In general, it may be remarked on this subject, that no political problem is less susceptible of a precise solution than that which relates to the number most convenient for a representative legislature . . .

. . . The truth is, that in all cases a certain number at least seems to be necessary to secure the benefits of free consultation and discussion, and to guard against too easy a combination for improper purposes; as, on the other hand, the number ought at most to be kept within a certain limit, in order to avoid the confusion and intemperance of a multitude . . .

. . . It is said, in the first place, that **so small a number cannot be safely trusted with so much power** . . .

. . . **I take for granted** here what I shall, in answering the fourth objection, hereafter show, **that the number of representatives will be augmented from time to time in the manner provided by the Constitution** . . .

. . . Within three years a census is to be taken, when **the number may be augmented to one for every thirty thousand inhabitants**; and within every successive period of ten years the census is to be renewed, and **augmentations may continue to be made under the above limitation** . . .

. . . **The true question to be decided then is, whether the smallness of the number . . . be dangerous to the public liberty?** . . .

. . . I am unable to conceive that **the State legislatures**, which must feel so many motives to watch, and which possess so many means of counteracting, the federal legislature, would fail either to detect or to defeat a conspiracy of the latter against the liberties of their common constituents . . .

What change of circumstances, time, and a fuller population of our country may produce, requires a prophetic spirit to declare, which **makes no part of my pretensions**. But judging from the circumstances now before us, and from the probable state of them within a moderate period of time, I must pronounce that the liberties of America cannot be unsafe in the number of hands proposed by the federal Constitution."[43]

Table 4: *United States Population Increase Over Time Compared to Number of Representatives in U.S. Congress*

Year	Total Population	Number of Representatives In House	How Many People Represented by Each Representative (Rounded)
1787*	*	65	
1790	3,929,214	105	37,000
1800	5,308,483	141	38,000
1810	7,239,881	181	40,000
1820	9,639,453	213	45,000
1830	12,866,020	240	54,000
1840	17,069,453	223	77,000
1850	23,191,876	234	99,000
1860	31,443,321	241	130,000
1870	39,818,449	292	136,000
1880	50,155,783	325	154,000
1890	62,947,714	356	177,000
1900	75,994,575	386	197,000
1910	**91,972,266**	**435**	**210,000**
1920	105,710,620	**435**	243,000
1930	122,775,046	**435**	282,000
1940	131,669,275	**435**	303,000
1950	151,325,798	**435**	348,000
1960	179,323,175	**435**	412,000
1970	203,302,031	**435**	467,000
1980	226,542,199	**435**	521,000
1990	248,718,301	**435**	572,000
2000	281,421,906	**435**	650,000
2010	**308,745,538**	**435**	**710,000**
2020**	341,400,000	?	785,000
2030**	373,500,000	?	849,000
2040**	405,700,000	?	933,000
2050**	439,000,000	?	1,009,000

*Based on original U.S. Constitution, Article I, section 2, paragraph 3.

**Projected (Source: U.S. Census Bureau, 1940 to 2010 Decennial Censuses; 2008 National Population Projections).

Reading the above passages, one is struck by the fact that at the time of ratification of the U.S. Constitution, many people were alarmed at turning over power to so few people. That was at a time when the contemplation was that there would be a new representative for each population growth of 30,000 people. Madison took "for granted" that the state legislatures, with Article V power to call a constitutional convention, would ensure our vote and representation would not become overly diluted over time. Experience has taught us that Madison's assumption was incorrect. Alexander Hamilton made a similar incorrect assumption in the Federalist Number 85, when he stated: "We may safely rely on the disposition of the state legislatures to erect barriers against the encroachments of the national authority."[44]

Since the Constitution was ratified, the size of the House of Representatives has grown a little over four times, while the population has grown one hundred times.

The Framers (perhaps the last somewhat honest generation of American politicians) actually acted as if the Size of Congress Amendment was part of the Constitution. Please consider Table 4: *United States Population Increase Over Time Compared to Number of Representatives in U.S. Congress.*

The Federalist Number 56 goes on to say:

"THE SECOND charge against the House of Representatives is, that it will be too small to possess a due knowledge of the interests of its constituents . . .

. . . It is a sound and important principle that the representative ought to be acquainted with the interests and circumstances of his constituents . . .

. . . **The foresight of the Convention has accordingly taken great care that the progress of population may be accompanied with a proper increase of the representative branch in government** . . .

> **. . . [T]he House of Representatives . . . seems to give the fullest assurance that a representative for every thirty thousand inhabitants will render the latter [The House of Representatives] both a safe and competent guardian of the interests which will be confided to it."[45]**

In the Federalist Number 58, Madison emphasizes that the duty to apportion under Article I includes both geographical apportionment (what we now call redistricting,) and **augmentation** of representatives as the population grows:

> **"The unequivocal objects of these regulations are, first, to readjust, from time to time, the apportionment of representatives** to the number of inhabitants, under the single exception that each State shall have one representative at least; **secondly, to augment the number of representatives** at the same periods under the sole limitation, that the whole number shall not exceed one for every thirty thousand inhabitants."[46]

When in 1920 the United States Congress failed to keep the ratio of voters to each representative within a meaningful range, Congress acted unconstitutionally in two ways. Congress failed in its duty under Article IV, Section 4 of the Constitution to provide the states with a republican form of government[47], because representation has become so diluted that fewer and fewer voters have access to their representative and representatives can no longer be expected to know the various needs of the people in their district. Congress also failed to continue to apportion pursuant to Article I, Section 2, paragraph 3. Apportionment does not mean only rearranging the geography of the districts. It also means to increase (augment) the representatives in the House as the population grows.

With the lessons of experience, we now see that the original failure was the failure to continue working the problem after the original Size of Congress Amendment fell short of the ratifications needed to become part of the Bill of Rights. One of the primary reasons Congress is no longer responsive to public opinion is that the American people have forgotten about the necessity in a republic not to dilute each individual's vote to the extent we have. Secondarily this means we have failed to use our check and balance of an Article V constitutional convention against corrupt government or government which is incompetent to the task of representation.

American citizens need to ask themselves whether they really feel comfortable with 546 people (535 elected Congresspersons, 1 President and 1 Vice-President, and 9 Supreme Court justices) making decisions for the nearly third of a billion of the rest of us. As to the size of the House of Representatives, the original Size of Congress Amendment has outlived its usefulness, and did so in the 1820's. The only solution which presents itself (without completely starting from scratch) is to divide Congress into three separate divisions instead of two, going from a bicameral legislature to a type of tricameral legislature.

With how far education and human knowledge have advanced since the Constitution was written, the biased view of the Framers that working class people are unable to grasp matters of national and international concern is not really an issue. With equal opportunity to education, the working classes are just as intelligent as the wealthy, and could and should have a seat at the Congressional table in order to participate in our own governance.

Members of the House of Representatives represent so many people that the interests of huge amounts of Americans are not even known to them. Congress is operating on incomplete information. George Mason, one of the delegates at the end of the 1787 Convention who refused to sign the Constitution, wrote:

> In the House of Representatives there is not the substance but the shadow only of representation; which can never produce proper information in the legislature, or inspire confidence in the people; the laws will therefore be generally made by men little concerned in, and unacquainted with their effects and consequences.[48]

There are many minority religions that have no one representing them in Congress. The homeless and disabled have no true representatives. Independents, the youth and most of the working class are basically taxed without representation. If any groups have the right to claim the Tea Party name, it is these groups. (See Graph 2: *Nationwide Political Affiliation*, at page 54.)

Interestingly, the size of congress was an issue most dear to George Washington. George Washington was not only the first President of the United States, he was the President of the United States' only constitutional convention.[49] With respect to his leadership of the 1787 Convention, George Washington spoke little and allowed the delegates to do their work.[50] It was an example of a leader knowing when to let the membership lead.

On September 15, 1787, the final version of the United States Constitution had been agreed to. The delegates gathered on September 17, 1787 to sign the fancy original document on parchment paper. The September 15, 1787 version included language that there would not be more than one representative for every 40,000 people. In a last minute doubt, delegate Nathaniel Gorham of Massachusetts stated that to lessen objections to the Constitution, the number should be 30,000.[51] George Washington, who had remained steadfastly neutral throughout the 1787 Constitutional Convention, in his capacity as President of the Convention, could not contain himself but spoke out and agreed that the change should be made to thirty thousand people per representative.[52] He expressed how many members felt, that <u>too few representatives would lead to insufficient security for the rights and interests of the people.</u>[53]

George Washington acknowledged that the smallish nature of the legislature was a concern, and thought it important enough to break with his neutral stance as President of the Constitutional Convention and speak up and support the change to 30,000 people per representative. The assembly unanimously approved the change to 30,000 people per representative before signing the newly proposed Constitution.[54]

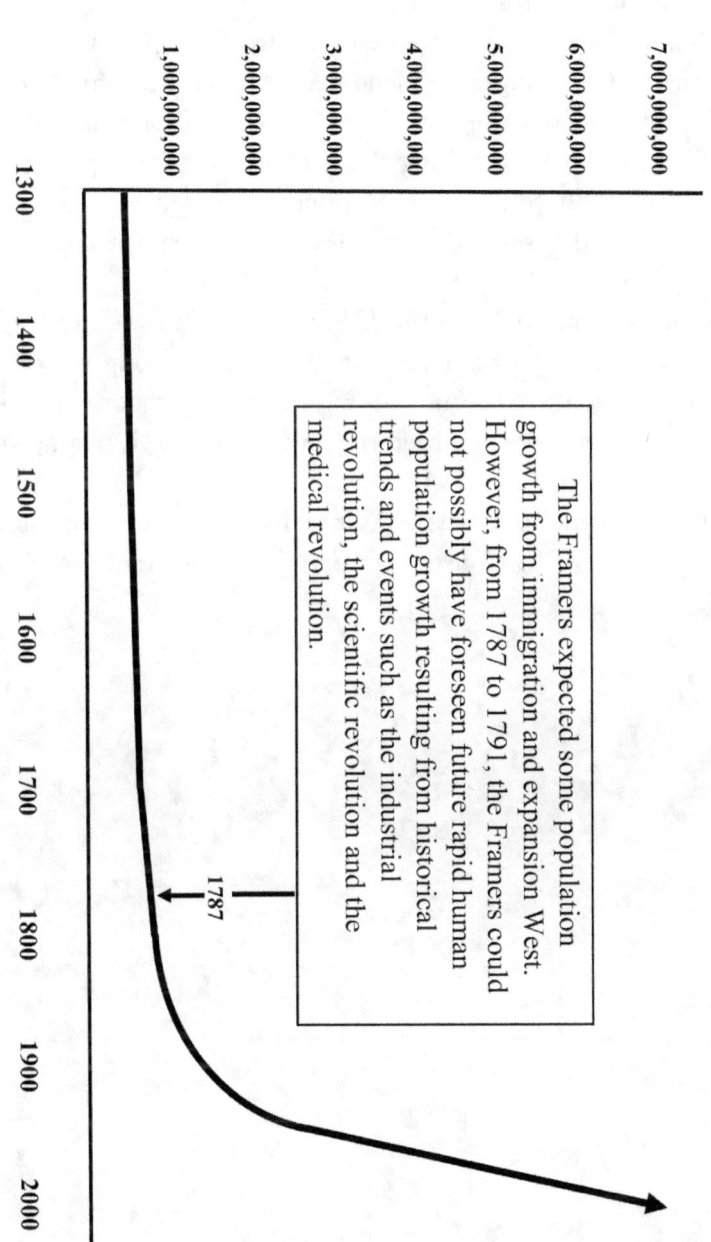

Graph 1: World Population, 1300-2000

The Framers expected some population growth from immigration and expansion West. However, from 1787 to 1791, the Framers could not possibly have foreseen future rapid human population growth resulting from historical trends and events such as the industrial revolution, the scientific revolution and the medical revolution.

1787

7,000,000,000
6,000,000,000
5,000,000,000
4,000,000,000
3,000,000,000
2,000,000,000
1,000,000,000

1300   1400   1500   1600   1700   1800   1900   2000

Years A.D.

The First Congress meant to improve such representation clause in 1789, but as discussed herein, the meaning of the proposed first amendment, the Size of Congress Amendment, changed in conference committee. Even if ratified it would have reached the end of its usefulness by the mid-1820's. It is not surprising the issue was overlooked. The Founding Generation simply could not have anticipated world population growth to have expanded the way it did after 1800. (See Graph 1: *World Population, 1300-2000*, at page 25.)

To update and improve the U.S. Constitution, we must update and improve the Size of Congress Amendment by moving to some type of tricameral legislature. Because it is highly unlikely that the U.S. Congress will act to curtail its own power, the only possibility is to amend the U.S. Constitution through a constitutional convention called by two thirds of the states, pursuant to Article V. As it turns out, the other major structural flaw within the U.S. Constitution is within the Article V Convention Clause itself.

The Framers Rushed the Constitutional Convention Clause at the End of the 1787 Convention

*"Col. Mason urged the necessity of such a provision. The plan now to be formed will certainly be defective, as the Confederation has been found on trial to be. **Amendments therefore will be necessary, and it will be better to provide for them, in an easy, regular and Constitutional way than to trust to chance and violence. It would be improper to require the consent of the Natl. Legislature, because they may abuse their power, and refuse their consent on that very account. The opportunity for such an abuse, may be the fault of the Constitution calling for amendment."***

(COLONEL GEORGE MASON, CONSTITUTIONAL
CONVENTION, JUNE 11, 1787, EMPHASIS ADDED.)

ARTICLE V OF THE UNITED States Constitution contains the Amendment Clause of the Constitution. Within the Amendment Clause is the Constitutional Convention Clause (set forth in bold below.)

Article V, United States Constitution

The Congress, whenever two thirds of both Houses shall deem it necessary, shall propose Amendments to this Constitution, or **on the**

Application of the Legislatures of two thirds of the several States, shall call a Convention for proposing Amendments, which, in either Case, **shall be valid to all Intents and Purposes, as Part of this Constitution, when ratified by the Legislatures of three fourths of the several States, or by Conventions in three fourths thereof, as the one or the other Mode of Ratification may be proposed by the Congress;** Provided that no Amendment which may be made prior to the Year One thousand eight hundred and eight shall in any Manner affect the first and fourth Clauses in the Ninth Section of the first Article; and that no State, without its Consent, shall be deprived of its equal Suffrage in the Senate.

The clause is an example of constitutional malpractice. **The Constitutional Convention Clause fails to provide any rules or procedures for choosing delegates** to a future convention. The final revisions to the Amendment Clause were not made until the end of the last work day of the 1787 Convention, on September 15, 1787.[1] The clause was not thoroughly thought through, and the delegates were anxious to finish their work and go home.[2] As a result, the Convention Clause is one of the deep structural defects in the U.S. Constitution.

When the Ninth Amendment and Tenth Amendment were made part of the U.S. Constitution (when the Bill of Rights was ratified,) the American people were left in a Devil's Loop with regard to the choosing of delegates to future constitutional conventions. (See Illustration 1: *The Devil's Loop of the American Constitution*, at page 3.) Per the Constitution itself, only the People sitting in Convention have the power to make rules and procedures for a constitutional convention. If we have agreement on how to choose the delegates to a future constitutional convention, the convention itself could establish its own rules. However, without clear rules for choosing delegates, We the People have no ability to start the work of an Article V convention, even after two-thirds of the state legislatures vote for one.

The Framers' intent that the sovereignty of the United States ultimately rests with its people, rather than with the legislatures of its state governments, is evidenced by the Preamble of the U.S. Constitution, which starts with the words "We The People." The Preamble makes a distinction which is crucial in Convention Clause analysis. When the Committee of Detail produced a first written draft of a constitution on August 6, 1787, and up to September 8, 1787, the Preamble read as follows:

> "We the people of the States of New Hampshire, Massachusetts, Rhode-Island and Providence Plantations, Connecticut, New-York, New-Jersey, Pennsylvania, Delaware, Maryland, Virginia, North-Carolina, South-Carolina, and Georgia, do ordain, declare, and establish the following Constitution for the Government of Ourselves and our Posterity."[3]

Near the end of the 1787 Constitutional Convention, on September 8, 1787, a Committee of Style & Arrangement was formed to incorporate and reorganize all of the changes made since the August 6, 1787 Committee of Detail report. When the Committee of Style and Arrangement (of which James Madison was a member[4]) produced its report on September 12, 1787, the Preamble had been re-written to what we know today:

> "WE, the People of the United States, in order to form a more perfect union, to establish justice, insure domestic tranquility, provide for the common defence, promote the general welfare, and secure the blessings of liberty to ourselves and our posterity, do ordain and establish this Constitution for the United States of America."[5]

The change from "We the people of the states, etc." to "We the People of the United States, etc." is key to interpreting the Article V convention power. It reflects an intent that the Article V convention power remain with the People rather than with state legislatures. An interaction between Patrick Henry and James Madison, at the Virginia ratifying convention which took place in 1788, further establishes the intent of the framers and the ratifiers of the Constitution. On June 4, 1788, Patrick Henry (of "Give me liberty or give me death!" fame) asked of those gentlemen who had served as delegates to the Constitutional Convention of 1787:

> "What right had they to say, *We, the people?* My political curiosity, exclusive of my anxious solicitude for the public welfare, leads me to ask, Who authorized them to speak the language of, *We, the people*, instead of, *We, the states?* States are the characteristics and the soul of a confederation. If the states be not the agents of this compact, it must be one great, consolidated, national government, of the people of all the states."[6]

James Madison, known as the father of the Constitution, had the benefit of two nights' rest before he responded on June 6, 1788:

> "Should all the states adopt it, **it will be then a government established** by the thirteen states of America, not through the intervention of the legislatures, but **by the people at large.** In this particular respect, **the distinction between the existing and proposed governments is very material. The existing system has been derived from the dependent derivative authority of the legislatures of the states; whereas this is derived from the superior power of the people.**"[7]

Madison emphasized the point in writing in the Federalist Number 49:

> "[T]he people are the only legitimate fountain of power, and it is from them that the constitutional charter, under which the several branches of government hold their power, is derived . . ."[8]

In George Washington's Farewell Address, he stated:

> "The basis of our political systems is the right of the people to make and to alter their constitutions of government. But the Constitution which at any time exists, until changed by an explicit and authentic act **of the whole people**, is sacredly obligatory upon all. The very idea of **the power and the right of the people** to establish government presupposes the duty of every individual to obey the established government."[9]

The problem is that the People do not have the right to make and alter their Constitution, because even if two-thirds of the state legislatures vote for the call of the convention, the convention cannot begin until delegates are chosen. Neither the U.S. Congress not the state legislatures have any power over a convention other than what is delegated by the Constitution itself. The intent of the Framers was clear that the People, not the state legislatures, have the power to act in constitutional convention under Article V. This power includes deciding the rules for choosing delegates to such a convention, and the Ninth and Tenth Amendments direct the interpretation of the Convention Clause to this result.

Ninth Amendment, United States Constitution

The enumeration in the Constitution, of certain rights, shall not be construed to deny or disparage others retained by the people.[10]

Tenth Amendment, United States Constitution

The powers not delegated to the United States by the Constitution, nor prohibited by it to the States, are reserved to the States respectively, or to the people.

This leaves us in a Devil's Loop (see Illustration 1, at page 3.) Rules cannot be made for the convention until delegates are chosen, and rules for choosing delegates cannot be made until there is a convention. It is not the ability to "call" for the convention which provides the power to the People, but rather the ability to sit down, do work and ultimately propose constitutional amendments. Without a remedy to enforce a right, you have no such right. Without a remedy to choose delegates to an Article V convention, the American people have no right to a constitutional convention and no peaceful pathway to correct corrupted government.

The most important consideration to spur us to call for a constitutional convention is the need for a peaceful, non-violent avenue to constitutional change. One of the primary considerations at the Constitutional Convention of 1787 with respect to the amendment clause was stated by Colonel George Mason of Virginia on June 11, 1787:

> "**Amendments** therefore will be necessary, and it will be **better to provide for them, in an easy, regular and Constitutional way than to trust to chance and violence**. It would be improper to require the consent of the Natl. Legislature, because they may abuse their power, and refuse their consent on that very account. **The opportunity for such an abuse, may be the fault of the Constitution** calling for amendment."[1]

Unfortunately, between June 11, 1787 and September 15, 1787, when the Article V Convention Clause was inserted into the text, Mason's concern was not properly addressed. (See Appendix 3: *Article V Revision History During Constitutional Convention*.) His warning was that if the clause allowing for amendment to the constitution is defective, it will allow abuse at the federal level to continue. It appears that his warning was not heeded, and in fact a defect in the Convention Clause is preventing the nation from using its primary check and balance against corrupted government – a convention for the purpose of proposing amendments to the Constitution. Without such check and balance, we are left to what Mason referred to as "chance and violence." Such chance and violence clearly pose a threat to the existence to our continuing nation.

James Madison, in the Federalist Number 43, acknowledged that if the Constitution was too difficult to amend, it would "perpetuate its discovered faults."[12] The Framers expected us to work to amend the Constitution when defects are discovered through experience.[13] As set forth in Chapter 2, we know through experience that due to the early failure to ratify an amendment that would increase representatives with increased population size, the United States of America is no longer a republic. Because the Constitutional Convention Clause is defective, and the Constitution is too difficult to amend, the "discovered fault" of failing to pass an adequate Size of Congress Amendment will continue to grow and become worse as our population continues to grow. On top of this concern is the nation's gradual shift to an unbalanced power structure which worsens things like wealth inequality and incompetent government, where people begin to take matters into their own hands.

Because the Convention Clause in our Constitution was a "rush job," and is defective in that there are no provisions for how delegates are chosen or how many delegates from each state may attend and vote, it does not serve the function of guarding against a constitutional crisis and social unrest. We risk a true breakdown in the system and all of the mischief and violence that would come with it.

The responsibility of beginning the process of amending the U.S. Constitution when a defect is detected lies with either the U.S. Congress or with the state legislatures. When the U.S. Congress is corrupt or will not act, there is only one pathway to amendment, through a constitutional convention called by two-thirds of the states' legislatures. However, if that path is defective, there is no peaceful pathway to amending the U.S. Constitution. One of the basic promises for the People giving up their power to "representatives" is broken, throwing the whole system into disarray and chaos as more and more people realize there is no power of the People to alter their own Constitution. This is a dangerous situation and should not be ignored by those who have taken an oath to support and defend the U.S. Constitution.

The Committee of Style and Arrangement of the original Constitutional Convention was appointed September 8, 1787, and returned its report including the near final version of the Constitution on September 12, 1787.[14] The Committee's report included an amendment clause that did not provide for a constitutional convention. The Amendment Clause of the Constitution, Article V, was literally the last clause revised at the end of the last work day, Saturday, September 15, 1787.[15] Because the entire project nearly unraveled near the end, the delegates to the only U.S. constitutional convention in history abandoned the tradition of the Senate at the end of the Constitutional Convention. (In other words, they allowed the clause to become part of the Constitution without much thought or debate.) The delegates, fearful of losing four months of cooperation, good fortune and compromise, agreed to an imperfect Convention Clause and moved to finalize the document. What we are left with has been described as a "hopelessly confused morass" and is a constitutional crisis waiting to happen.[16]

FARRAND'S THE RECORDS OF THE FEDERAL CONVENTION OF 1787

In 1911, law professor Max Farrand edited and published, through the Yale University Press, The Records of the Federal Convention of 1787 in a three-volume set. Farrand compiled the notes of the various delegates to the Constitutional Convention, combined them with the records of the official Journal, and placed them in chronological order for ease of study. The work is out of copyright and easily available over the internet for download for anyone to study. Readers are encouraged to download The Records of the Federal Convention of 1787 and confirm the history which will be set forth herein. (See Appendix 3: *Article V Revision History During Constitutional Convention* and Appendix 4: *Additional Notes from the Constitutional Convention Re: the Topic of a Constitutional Convention*.)

MAY 29, 1787 – THE VIRGINIA PLAN

Article V of the Constitution started as a very simple concept. The Virginia Plan was a collection of fifteen resolutions by the Virginia delegation to the Constitutional Convention.[17] Governor Edmund Randolph of Virginia proposed The Virginia Plan to the other convention delegates on May 29, 1787.[18] The thirteenth provision, for amendment, stated simply:

"Resolved that provision ought to be made for the amendment of the Articles of Union whensoever it shall seem necessary, and that the assent of the National Legislature ought not to be required thereto."[19]

Such proto-clause did not mention a convention, provided no guidelines as to which body would propose and which body would consent to the amendments of the Constitution, or what percentage margin of vote would be needed to propose or ratify amendments. This proto-clause also introduces the concept of being able to amend the Constitution without the national government being able to block amendments. While not stated expressly, the proto-clause suggests the ability to provide a check and balance against corrupt or incompetent national government.

JUNE 5, 1787

The first time Resolution 13 was mentioned at the Convention was on June 5, 1787. The entirety of the discussion in the record that day regarding Resolution 13 follows:

"Mr. Pinkney doubted the propriety or necessity of it.

Mr. Gerry favored it. The novelty & difficulty of the experiment requires periodical revision. The prospect of such a revision would also give intermediate stability to the Govt. Nothing had yet happened in the States where this provision existed to prove its impropriety. – The Proposition was postponed for further consideration."[20]

JUNE 11, 1787

When the proposed clause was brought before the Convention again on June 11, 1787, the discussion was as follows:

"<Resolution 13> for amending the national Constitution hereafter without consent of Natl. Legislature <being> considered, several members did not see the necessity of the <Resolution> at all, nor the propriety of making the consent of the Natl. Legisl. unnecessary.

Col. Mason urged the necessity of such a provision. The plan now to be formed will certainly be defective, as the Confederation has been found on trial to be. Amendments therefore will be necessary, and it will be better to provide for them, in an easy, regular and Constitutional way than to trust to chance and violence. It would be improper to require the consent of the Natl. Legislature, because they may abuse their power, and refuse their consent on that very account. The opportunity for such an abuse, may be the fault of the Constitution calling for amendment.

Mr. Randolph <enforced> these arguments.

The words, "without requiring the consent of the Natl. Legislature" were postponed. The other provision in the clause passed nem. con."[21] ["nem. con." means without opposition]

The most the Convention could agree to by this date was that there should be some provision to amend the Constitution. The delegates begin discussing the concept of a check and balance allowing amendment to the Constitution by a means outside the national government. Colonel Mason makes the excellent point that if the amendment clause is not sufficient it would probably lead to eventual violence due to the U.S. Congress refusing to make necessary amendments while the people have no true path around Congress.

The simple provision for amendment carried through to the report of the Committee of the Whole House on June 13, 1787, when the resolution was renumbered from 13 to 17.[22] What the assembly is basically doing at this point of the Convention with respect to the amendment clause is to "punt." They are placing a low priority on the issue while they deal with the terms that will determine if the 1787 Constitutional Convention would be successful, such as how to balance between big states and small states and how to address the issue of slavery.

AUGUST 6, 1787 – DRAFT OF COMMITTEE OF DETAIL

The fact that the men at the Convention placed low priority on the amendment clause is reflected in the fact that it was not addressed again in Convention until the delegates were ready to begin preparing a first draft. The first two months of the convention were spent discussing general principles.[23] Near the end of July, the Convention adjourned for ten days to allow a Committee of Detail, consisting of five delegates, to prepare the first written draft of the Constitution.[24]

The Committee of Detail worked between July 26 and August 3 or 4, 1787, and reported to the Convention on August 6, 1787.[25] The five men on the Committee of Detail, delegates John Rutledge of South Carolina, Edmund Randolph of Virginia, Nathaniel Gorham of Massachusetts, Oliver Ellsworth of Connecticut, and James Wilson of Pennsylvania, finally had an opportunity to address the amendment clause in committee. We have no record of the discussions of the Committee of Detail, only a number of written drafting documents.[26] The first revision was quite rough, but introduces the concept of using a Constitutional Convention:

> "An alteration may be effected in the articles of union, on application of two thirds of the state legislatures to the Natl. Leg. they call a Convn. to revise or alter ye Articles of Union."[27]

The second revision by The Committee of Detail to the amendment clause resulted in the following language:

> "This Constitution ought to be amended whenever such Amendment shall become necessary; and on the Application of the Legislatures of two thirds of the States in the Union, the Legislature of the United States shall call a Convention for that Purpose."[28]

When the Committee of Detail provided the Convention with the first written draft of the U. S. Constitution on August 6, 1787, the language of the amendment clause, renumbered again as Roman numeral XIX, read as follows:

"On the application of the Legislatures of two thirds of the States in the Union, for an amendment of this Constitution, the Legislature of the United States shall call a Convention for that purpose."[29]

The final version of the Constitution was signed by most of the delegates on September 17, 1787.[30] On August 6, just a little more than a month before, we finally see the beginnings of what the final amendment clause will look like. However, the final version will be close to 12 lines long, while this initial written version is only three lines long. There are no standards, rules or procedures for future conventions, and Congress does not have the ability to propose amendments. There is no mention of any need for the state legislatures to ratify a future convention's work.

With a rough draft in hand, the Convention began to go over the document and revise, clause by clause. Even though they have the rough language of an amendment clause on August 6, 1787, they do not actually discuss the amendment clause until August 30, 1787, just two and one-half weeks before the end of the Convention. The discussion is short:

"Art: XIX taken up.
    Mr. Govr. Morris suggested that the Legislature should be left at liberty to call a Convention, whenever they please.
    The art: was agreed to nem: con: [without opposition]"[31]

SEPTEMBER 10, 1787

A Committee of Style and Arrangement was appointed on September 8, 1787, for the purpose of rearranging the Convention's work into a near final draft.[32] The committee included William Samuel Johnson of Connecticut, Alexander Hamilton of New York, Gouverneur Morris of Pennsylvania, James Madison of Virginia and Rufus King of Massachusetts. The second written draft was presented to the entirety of the Convention on September 12, 1787.[33]

On Monday, September 10, 1787 (just one week before the Constitution will be signed, and just five days before the final day for revisions,) the Convention starts to focus upon and discuss the amendment clause (Please see Appendix 3: *Article V Revision History During Constitutional Convention*.)

Elbridge Gerry of Massachusetts moves to reopen discussion regarding what was then Article XIX. Gerry expresses concern that with the Supremacy Clause in the Constitution, some of the states could "subvert" the other states.[34] Alexander Hamilton of New York then seconds the motion, but with a differing view that the clause basically gave the states too much power to subvert the federal government.[35] Then,

"Mr Madison remarked on the vagueness of the terms, 'call a Convention for the purpose.' as sufficient reason for reconsidering the article. How was a Convention to be formed? by what rule decide? what the force of its acts?"[36]

With just one week left before the Convention ends, this is the first discussion of any real substance regarding the Amendment Clause. When Madison speaks, it is a warning to the entire delegation that they should establish basic rules and procedure for the convention clause. **"How was a Convention to be formed? by what rule decide? what the force of its acts?"**

The Convention then agrees to reconsider the clause. Mr. Sherman proposes that 1) the national legislature also can propose amendments and 2) a requirement that states consent to any proposed amendments. Mr. Wilson moves to set the ratification bar at two-thirds of the states, which loses by just one vote. Mr. Wilson moves again, this time to require three-quarters of the states for ratification of an amendment. It passes without opposition.[37]

Then Madison makes a motion which eliminates the Convention Clause altogether. Other than Madison's questions regarding convention rules and procedure, there has still been no convention-wide discussion regarding the convention alternative. Madison proposes new language which gives both the national legislature and the state legislatures the ability to propose amendments. Madison's proposal eliminates the convention option for <u>proposing</u> amendments completely, without any discussion whatsoever about its removal.[38]

Before a vote could be taken on Madison's new proposal, John Rutledge of South Carolina **"said he never could agree to give a power by which the articles relating to slaves might be altered by the states not interested in that property and prejudiced against it."**[39] As a result, a sort of "hidden" slave clause is added to the Constitution. Many people read Article V today and skim over the new addition to the clause made on September 10, 1787, namely that no amendments would be made to the fourth and fifth sections of the seventh article for at least twenty years. The Convention delegates carefully euphemized (softened) the language in the Constitution regarding slavery.[40] The fourth and fifth sections of what was on that day article seven are two examples. Those two sections became clauses one and four of section nine of Article I.[41] The first clause guaranteed the slave states the right to import slaves for at least another twenty years, while the second prevented against the slave states being taxed at the rate of 100% of the "slave count," instead requiring taxes to be based on The Three-Fifths Clause.[42]

The amendment article, as revised, now reads:

XIX.

The Legislature of the United States, whenever two thirds of both Houses shall deem necessary, or on the application of two thirds of the Legislatures of the several States, shall propose amendments to this Constitution which shall be valid to all intents and purposes as parts thereof, when the same shall have been ratified by three fourths at least of the Legislatures of the several States, or by Conventions in three fourths thereof, as one or the other mode of ratification may be proposed by the Legislature of the United-States: Provided that no amendments which may be made prior to the year 1808, shall in any manner affect the 4th and 5th Sections of article the 7th[43]

In the report of the Committee of Style on September 12, 1787, the amendment clause is renumbered as Article V, with more concise language but the same meaning.[44]

SEPTEMBER 14, 1787

September 14, 1787 was a Friday. The convention worked, but did not discuss Article V on this day.

We know that the Framers of the U.S. Constitution had a celebration dinner on Monday, September 17, 1787, after they had finished their work.[45] What most people, including lawyers and judges, do not know is that there was another big celebration dinner on Friday, September 14, 1787, before the delegates had finished revising Article V. The party was apparently thrown by the First Troop Philadelphia City Cavalry in honor of George Washington. While it is not clear that people got drunk, there is a bill for the Friday night dinner at the City Tavern, Philadelphia showing a sizeable amount of alcoholic products consumed.[46]

We also know that the next day, September 15, was the last work day of the 1787 Convention. It was probably the longest work day of the Convention, not adjourning until 6:00 p.m. on a Saturday.[47] For the first three months of the Convention, work hours were apparently somewhat irregular.[48] On August 18, 1787, with still a month's work to go, Mr. Rutledge "remarked on the length of the Session, the probable impatience of the public and the extreme anxiety of many members of the Convention to bring the business to an end . . ."[49] As a result of his motion, the Convention agreed to meet precisely at 10:00 a.m. and not adjourn until at least 4:00 p.m.[50] These six hour days were apparently taxing, and on August 24, 1787, a motion passed unanimously to start at 10:00 a.m. and adjourn at 3:00 p.m.[51]

Working an eight-hour day on the last day of work, after a night of some drinking, and waiting until near the end of the day to discuss the Convention Clause, it is not at all surprising that the delegates would not have completely thought through the clause. The biases of the members against a second convention until the nation stabilized would also have influenced the main leaders not to push too hard for a clear path to a second convention. The fact that the delegates were anticipating the end of the Convention, along with these other factors, helps to explain why the Convention Clause would have been rushed and imperfect.

SEPTEMBER 15, 1787

The only meaningful discussion and debate regarding a constitutional convention comes at the very end of the 1787 Convention when the delegates are tired and are already anticipating the completion of their project. Even that discussion, on September 15, 1787, is brief, but apparently heated. (Please see Appendix 3: *Article V Revision History During Constitutional Convention.*) The first four paragraphs of that day's record regarding Article V are most relevant to the discussion of the Convention Clause:

> Mr. Sherman expressed his fears that three fourths of the States might be brought to do things fatal to particular States, as abolishing them altogether or depriving them of their equality in the Senate. He thought it reasonable that the proviso in favor of the States importing slaves should be extended so as to provide that no State should be affected in its internal police, or deprived of its equality in the Senate.
>
> Col: Mason thought the plan of amending the Constitution exceptionable & dangerous. **As the proposing of amendments is** in both the modes **to depend**, in the first immediately, and in the second, ultimately, **on Congress, no amendments of the proper kind would ever be obtained by the people, if the Government should become oppressive,** as he verily believed would be the case.
>
> Mr. Govr. Morris & Mr. Gerry **moved to amend the article so as to require a Convention on application of ⅔ of the States.**
>
> Mr Madison did not see why Congress would not be as much **bound** to propose amendments applied for by two thirds of the States as to call a Convention on the like application. He saw no

objection however against providing for a Convention for the purpose of amendments, except **only that difficulties might arise as
to the form, the quorum etc. which in Constitutional regulations ought to be as much as possible avoided.**[52]

The actual discussion about the Convention Clause is brief. Colonel
Mason is concerned that the People would not ever be able to amend the
Constitution if Congress should "become oppressive." Gouverneur Morris
and Elbridge Gerry move to insert the Convention Clause. Madison then
establishes that it would be a mandatory duty (not a power) for Congress
to call a convention if sufficient states demanded it. **He again warns the
Convention that "difficulties might arise as to the form, the quorum
etc which in Constitutional regulations ought to be as much as possible avoided."** Madison's warning is essentially ignored and the delegates
vote to include a convention clause without opposition.

We then see a flurry of quick motions before the end of the 1787
Convention. At this point, Madison seems to be getting impatient and
states: "Begin with these special provisos, and every State will insist on
them, for their boundaries, exports etc."[53]

Sherman makes the somewhat bizarre motion to strike out the amendment article, Article V, altogether, which loses. Then,

> **Mr. Govr Morris moved to annex a further proviso – "that no
> State, without its consent shall be deprived of its equal suf-
> frage in the Senate"**
>   **This motion being dictated by the circulating murmurs of
> the small States was agreed to without debate, no one oppos-
> ing it, or on the question, saying no.**[54]

At this point the convention delegates simply abandon good practice of fully
discussing the issue. It seems fairly obvious when reading the record that the
small states and the slave states were able to get additional concessions under an
implied threat that they were willing to risk the good of the new nation unless

they got their way. The other states "caved" and that was basically the end of the Convention. Delegates Mason, Randolph and Gerry set forth their objections on the record, then the Convention voted to approve the new Constitution as drafted and ordered it to be prepared in final for signing.[55]

Altogether, the discussion about the Amendment Clause at the Convention makes up less than seven pages of text. The discussion about the Convention Clause within the Amendment Clause is about two pages, including Madison's warnings about the danger of not setting up rules and procedures for future conventions. (See Appendix 3.)

Not Only is Congress Corrupt, So Are Its Lawyers (Which We Pay For)

For nearly fifty years, some members of the U.S. Congress have assumed that the U.S. legislative branch may limit the American people's constitutional convention rights by proposing constitutional convention procedures bills which purport to rewrite the terms of the U.S. Constitution. Sometimes, the Congressional research attorneys provide support to such Congressional overreach by providing inaccurate research opinions. The danger to the American people is that we are left with an ignorant Congress that risks violence and upheaval because they are not informed enough to understand the hazards of failing to act to correct constitutional defects.

A prime example of the Congressional Research Service's incompetent analysis from two of the more recent Congressional Research Service reports is the following statement: "The Article V Convention for proposing amendments was the subject of considerable debate and forethought in the Philadelphia Convention of 1787."[56] The statement is false. As demonstrated in this chapter, there was very little debate at the 1787 Constitutional Convention regarding the Convention Clause, despite James Madison warning the delegates twice that the procedural architecture should be agreed upon within the terms of the Constitution itself.

As established in this chapter, the discussion of the Convention Clause was in no manner "the subject of considerable debate and forethought in the Philadelphia Convention of 1787." There was almost no discussion about the Convention Clause at the 1787 Convention. When the document came back from the Committee of Style and Arrangement, there was no provision for a constitutional convention. Literally, at the end of the 1787 Convention, the Convention Clause was reinserted but without serious discussion or thought. Nearly two-hundred thirty years later, we have still not had a constitutional convention under the "new" rules of the U.S. Constitution, in part due to the defect that the procedural architecture for an Article V convention is not yet built.

According to a June 17, 2015 New York Times article, the Congressional Research Service employs over 600 people and costs the American taxpayers over $100 million per year.[57] Congress is the public's fiduciary, and a fiduciary has the duty to not utilize its position to the detriment of its beneficiaries, in this case the American people. As stated in the beginning of this chapter, the Congressional Research Service is feeding Congress with wrong-headed ideas that Congress has the power to steal the People's convention rights by imposing limits on the convention process. Congress has no such power. Essentially, the American people are paying the attorney's fees of Congress which are used by Congress to breach its duties to the American people by making unconstitutional power grabs.

Simply put, the clause regarding the constitutional convention was a rush job and was bungled. No deep thought was put into the clause. It certainly was not "the subject of considerable debate and forethought in the Philadelphia Convention of 1787," as alleged by the Congressional Research Service (one wonders whether the research service was <u>instructed</u> to provide misleading information to Congress.) The botched Convention Clause is one of the primary reasons we have never had another constitutional convention for 228 years, despite a heavy need to utilize our primary check and balance against corrupt, ineffective and/or unbalanced government. This sets the country up for the real danger of not having a peaceful pathway to amend the Constitution, and increases the risk of violent unrest. It is an absolutely irresponsible position in which to leave ourselves.

CHAPTER 4

We are Overdue for a Constitutional Convention

"If we fail to deal now with the uncertainties of the convention method, we could be courting a constitutional crisis of grave proportions. We would be running the enormous risk that procedures for a national constitutional convention would have to be forged in time of divisive controversy and confusion when there would be a high premium on obstructive and result oriented tactics."

(ABA Special Constitutional Convention Study Committee, *Amendment of the Constitution by the Convention Method under Article V*, at p. 8 (1974).)

The quote above is over forty years old. That was when the American Bar Association put together a committee to study the relatively new legal discovery of that time that the Article V Convention Clause is flawed due to its failure to provide the basic framework for choosing delegates and starting the work of a constitutional convention. Instead of addressing the problem, however, the problem has been ignored and the American people are cut off from using our primary check and balance against an out of control government.

The primary reason that the convention alternative to amend the Constitution came about was the desire to have a <u>non-violent pathway to amend</u> if the U.S. Congress should not act.[1] If we do not preserve and defend the peaceful path to improve our government, we risk the union itself. Increasing population pressures, unequal economic opportunities and the recently developing terrorism risks create a volatile mix of elements that could make it nearly impossible to hold the country together if we should want a constitutional convention but cannot start one because of a flawed Article V Convention Clause.

While Article V does not require a reason to call a constitutional convention, out of the 1787 Convention come these main ideas about when to hold a constitutional convention:

* When a defect is discovered through experience;
* When the government is corrupt/oppressive/abusive;
* When Congress will not act to propose necessary amendments.[2]

All three elements currently exist. All three appear to be related.

DEFECT DISCOVERED THROUGH EXPERIENCE

Approximately one hundred years ago, the United States Congress abandoned two of its constitutional duties (see Chapter 2.) The first was to continue to add more representatives as the population grew.[3] The duty to "grow" the House of Representatives as the population grows was made explicit by James Madison in The Federalist Number 58:

> "THE remaining charge against the House of Representatives, which I am to examine, is grounded on a supposition that the number of members will not be augmented from time to time, as the progress of population may demand. **It has been admitted, that this objection, if well supported, would have great weight** . . . Within every successive term of ten years a census of inhabitants is to be repeated. **The unequivocal objects of these regulations are, first, to readjust, from time to time, the apportionment of representatives** to the number of inhabitants, under the single exception that each State shall have one representative at least;

secondly, to augment the number of representatives at the same periods . . ."[4]

Madison's argument that the system which he helped devise was sufficient to ensure that representatives in the House would be augmented as the population grows has turned out to be incorrect (See Table 4: *United States Population Increase Over Time Compared to Number of Representatives in U.S. Congress*, at page 20.) It is an error, and Article V was included in the Constitution to correct such errors. The Framers had no idea that human population would explode as it has after 1800 (See Graph 1: *World Population, 1300-2000*, at page 25.) Experience has taught us that the failure to augment representation with population growth is an error of omission involving the failure to complete the Bill of Rights, and particularly the failure to ratify some version of a Size of Congress Amendment.

For nearly one hundred years, we have not had an increase in the number of representatives representing us. When the Constitution was ratified, people believed they would be sharing a representative with about 30,000 people. Now, we share a "representative" with nearly 750,000 people. In about thirty-five years, we will share a "representative" with over one million people. Such does not meet the definition of a republic, which requires meaningful representation.[5] If the vast majority of us cannot even meet for a few minutes with our representative, then we do not have representation and are no longer a democratic republic. The duty to guarantee a republican form of government under Article IV, Section 4 of the Constitution is the second duty which the U.S. Congress abandoned when it failed to augment representation to keep up with population growth.

Because the U.S. Congress will not act to perform these essential constitutional duties, only one peaceful pathway is left to us to correct these errors – a constitutional convention called by two thirds of the state legislatures (34 of 50) pursuant to Article V of the U.S. Constitution.

In Chapter 3, we learned the general history of the Article V Convention Clause at the 1787 Constitutional Convention. Resolution 13 of The Virginia Plan, introduced to the 1787 Convention on May 29, 1787, contained the concept of the need for a way around Congress: "Resolved that provision ought to be made for the amendment of the Articles of Union whensoever it shall seem necessary, and that the assent of the National Legislature ought not to be required thereto."[6] This concept was adopted by the Committee of Detail in its August 6, 1787 report when they included a draft clause requiring a constitutional convention if two-thirds of the state legislatures apply for an amendment to the Constitution. The convention language was eliminated by a Madison motion on September 10, 1787, only to be resurrected with more specificity on the last work day of the Convention, September 15, 1787. On both September 10 and September 15, 1787, Madison warned the Convention delegates that at least some of the procedure regarding how to form a constitutional convention should be addressed.

We also learned that the Framers ended the 1787 Convention knowing that the Article V Convention Clause may be defective. Some might argue that Madison's comments at the Constitutional Convention were speculation. However, once again, experience has taught us that Article V is defective because it fails to provide skeletal rules for the forming of an Article V convention, and especially rules for choosing delegates to the convention. The Constitutional Convention Clause is really the only reason we can even call our system "of the People." If an Article V Convention can never be used because Article V is itself defective, or the defect can be manipulated by the wealthy and powerful, then we have no right as a free people to alter our form of government and our system is not "of the People."

Madison knew that the Constitutional Convention Clause was at least potentially defective because it did not provide rules and procedures for the convention process. Rules for the original 1787 Constitutional Convention were established by the Convention itself in the first few days of work.[7] Practically speaking, if there were pre-set rules for choosing delegates to a future convention, the delegates could establish rules and procedures for the convention at the beginning of and during the course of the convention. In fact, the Constitution assigns such power to the People, as such power is denied to the government.[8] The problem, once again, is that there are no rules for choosing delegates to such a convention, and therefore no way to begin the process whereby the rules could be proposed, debated and established through vote of the convention delegates. (See Illustration 1: *The Devil's Loop of the American Constitution*, at page 3.)

How to choose delegates for an Article V convention is only one of a host of problems with the Article V Convention Clause uncovered when our country twice came close to the thirty-four-state threshold for calling a constitutional convention. A dispute exists in legal scholarship about whether the state legislatures may limit an Article V convention to a single topic. Two movements attempting to bring about a constitutional convention for the purpose of only a single proposed amendment (as opposed to a general constitutional convention free to discuss the entire Constitution) uncovered a host of both actual and potential procedural problems within the Article V convention process.

The problem on each occasion was that the states voting for such convention sought a convention for the purpose of a single-topic convention. Legal scholars disagree whether it would be constitutional to hold a single-topic convention, though the weight of scholarly opinion is that such would be unconstitutional. The very fact that there is a dispute about one of the most important clauses in the U.S. Constitution is reason enough for the state legislatures to call an Article V Convention to clear up Article V itself, for if we wait too long it could be too late.[9]

There were two movements toward a constitutional convention in the 1960's, 1970's and 1980's. The first sought to overturn Supreme Court rulings establishing a "one person, one vote" rule for both houses of each state legislature. The second sought a convention to propose a balanced budget amendment.

In 1964, the U.S. Supreme Court issued two rulings that imposed upon all states a clear "one person, one vote" rule.[10] This prevented states from using a method for choosing state representatives other than "one person, one vote" for state legislatures. For example, a state might have one senator from each county, even though county population size varies widely. Such practice was eliminated by Supreme Court ruling. In response, states began to seek an Article V convention for the purpose of overturning the Supreme Court decisions and allowing one house of a state legislature to be apportioned on a basis other than population.[11]

From 1964 to 1969, thirty-three state legislatures voted for an Article V convention to overturn the Supreme Court cases.[12] As the state votes came nearer to the thirty-four needed, state legislatures realized that the Constitution probably does not allow the state legislatures or the U.S. Congress to limit an Article V convention in such manner.[13] As a result, several states rescinded their applications and the movement lost energy.[14]

The second major attempt took place from 1975-1983, seeking a balanced budget amendment.[15] Thirty-two states voted for an Article V convention for such purpose, again making the mistake that the Constitution would allow the states and Congress to limit the convention topics.[16] Once again, in fear of what some called a "runaway convention," states pulled back and effort toward a balanced budget amendment faded away (until recently.)[17]

Using the state movements toward an Article V convention as justification, the U.S. Congress, from 1967 to 1991, and through mostly Republican senators, began proposing legislation designed to limit and "thieve" the American People's convention rights.[18] Among the limitations, such senators attempted to limit future Article V conventions by:

- creating administrative red tape requiring Article V applications for a convention to comply with a list of requirements not mandated by Article V, such as the title of the resolution and the date adopted. This could be used as a "ticky tack" reason to reject an application and prevent the American People's check and balance against a corrupt Congress.
- declaring the applications for an Article V convention to be good for only four years, violating the Ninth and Tenth Amendments.
- allowing Congress to delay an Article V convention for a whole year, again a clear violation of the Ninth Amendment.
- usurping the People's right to decide rules and procedures for choosing delegates and weighting the process in favor of smaller populated states by forcing on the states an electoral college

standard, giving each state two extra delegates, in violation of the Fourteenth Amendment and the "one person/one vote" Supreme Court cases.

* forcing delegates to take an oath to propose amendments only in conformity to congressional resolution, another violation of the Ninth and Tenth Amendments.

* limiting a convention to one year duration, under Congress' control, another violation of the Ninth and Tenth Amendments.

* taking away the courts' power to judge and assigning it to Congress, unconstitutional in a number of ways.

* requiring Congress' approval of any proposed amendment, a violation of Article V itself.

* limiting the amount of time an amendment can be ratified by the states for convention generated amendment proposals, again in violation of the Ninth and Tenth Amendments.

* allowing the states to adopt rules and procedures for ratification contrary to constitutional standards, in contravention of the text of Article V and the Ninth and Tenth Amendments.[19]

Any one of these issues, if not worked out by the appropriate parties, can prevent an Article V convention from convening and would cut off the American people from one of the essential checks and balances in the U.S. Constitution. We have now learned from experience that Article V is vague as to the procedures for an Article V convention and that disputes over such procedures have the potential or even likelihood to prevent such a convention from ever occurring, even in the face of an extremely corrupt U.S. Government.

We have discussed the error of omission of failing to complete the Bill of Rights with an adequate Size of Congress Amendment which would give us meaningful representation. Such error is exacerbated as our population and problems continue to grow and state legislatures refuse to call for a constitutional convention. Article V was meant to be the peaceful path to correct such errors when Congress will not act. However, as alluded to by James Madison in The Federalist Number 43, when the Constitution is too difficult to amend, it will "perpetuate its discovered faults."[20]

The longer we as a nation wait to correct these defects, the greater the detrimental effect will be to our political, legal, economic and social systems. It makes no sense to wait. An Article V Convention must be called now, for if we wait, we risk disaster.

CORRUPT GOVERNMENT

Public perception of corrupt government has grown to an unacceptable level. In a November 2015 Pew Research Center Report, "Beyond Distrust: How Americans View Their Government," 77 percent of Americans report that "elected officials lose touch with the people quickly," 74 percent of Americans say that elected officials "don't care what people like me think," and 74 percent of Americans say that "elected officials put their own interests ahead of the country's."[21]

Various Gallup surveys support the Pew findings. The number of Americans seeing corruption as widespread in the country's government went from 67% in 2009 to 75% in 2015.[22] Forty-nine percent in 2015 see the federal government as posing "an immediate threat to the rights and freedoms of ordinary citizens," up from 30% in 2003.[23] Only thirty-eight percent of Americans trust the federal government to handle domestic matters in 2015, down from an average of 62% from 1972-2004.[24] Sixty percent of Americans think the U.S. Government has too much power.[25] Congress' approval rating is at an abysmal 13%[26], and does not show any sign of improving. Congresspersons tend to behave as if they are not aware that the American people do not approve of Congress' work (or lack thereof.)

The issue is more than perception, as real findings confirm the public's viewpoint. For example, through gerrymandering, the two political parties have stolen from the American people much of the real competitiveness in the representational system. While only 29% of Americans are Democrats, and 26% are Republicans, 42% of Americans are independent of the two parties but have almost no representatives in Congress.[27] (See Graph 2: *Nationwide Political Affiliation*.) Gerrymandering really does "game" the system in such a way as to favor incumbents and those with access to the two-party apparatus, which again means those with money.

Graph 2: Nationwide Political Affiliation (Self-Reported)

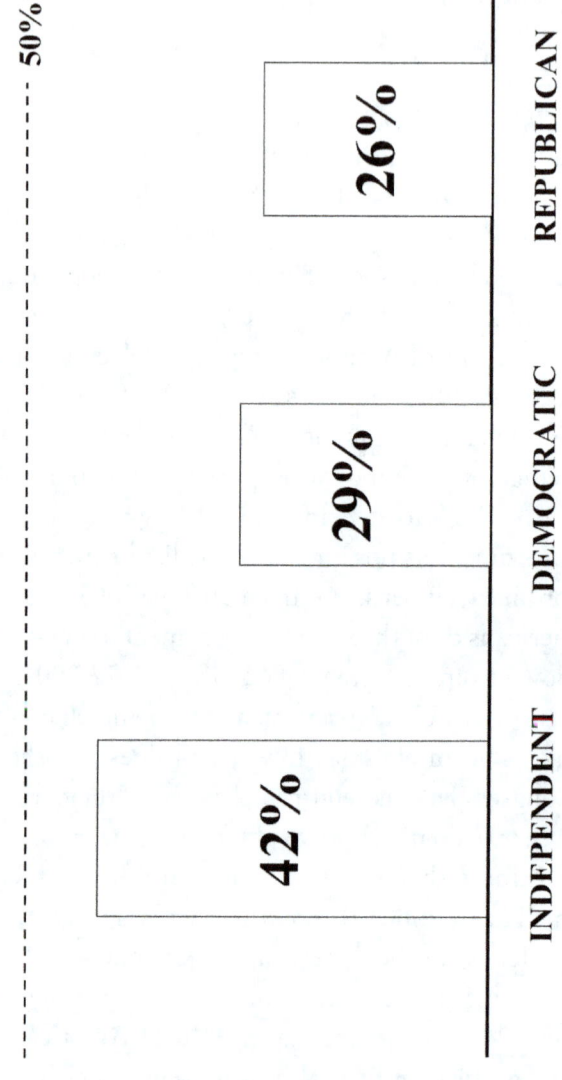

- - - - 50%

42%

29%

26%

INDEPENDENT DEMOCRATIC REPUBLICAN

(Jeffrey M. Jones, *Democratic, Republican Identification Near Historical Lows*, Gallup, January 11, 2016)

We now see a growing life span gap between the rich and poor. Where for men the gap in life span between rich and poor used to be six years, it is now fourteen years.[28] For women, the gap has gone from 4.7 years to 13 years.[29]

The economic system itself has continued to lose health. New businesses as a percentage of all businesses is one way to look at the health of an economy. When economic opportunities are poor, competent members of the working class are less likely to make the attempt to start a new business. Prior to 1980, nearly 15% of all businesses were new businesses.[30] By 2010, that figure was halved, to just over 7.5%. Facts like these correspond with the growth of extreme wealth inequality in our country. Over time, if the imbalances in the economy and economic opportunity are not addressed, we will begin to see reduced worker productivity, as the reality of a two-class system (owners vs. workers) sets in and workers refuse to be highly productive in a system where hard work no longer lifts an employee out of the working class.

To balance the economic system, however, we must balance the political system. This means reestablishing the foundations of our check and balance system, starting with using the check and balance of an Article V convention.

WHEN CONGRESS WILL NOT ACT TO PROPOSE NECESSARY AMENDMENTS

Per the Pew Research Center, 77 percent of the American people also "favor limiting the amount of money individuals and organizations can spend on campaigns and issues."[31] In 2010, in the case of *Citizens United v. Federal Election Commission*[32], the United States Supreme Court reversed one hundred years of limiting money in campaign finance in America, and instead turned our voting system into something closer to a "many dollars, one vote" system than a "one person, one vote" system. Politicians from both parties have given "lip service" to a constitutional amendment to overturn the *Citizens United* case, but the fact that there is no serious possibility of the U.S. Congress proposing such an amendment is one of voluminous pieces of evidence that Congress itself has become corrupt.

When Congress will not act to make necessary amendments, there is only one peaceful path to amendment – a constitutional convention brought about by vote of two-thirds of the state legislatures per Article V.

Gerrymandering is a reflection of state congressional self-dealing, and is highly undemocratic. In some parts of the country, state legislatures have been trying to make it harder for citizens to vote, again highly undemocratic. These matters will probably need to be addressed through constitutional amendment. The founders did not anticipate the growth of two political parties with such entrenched power. The Framers did not think about checks and balances against political parties that might become so powerful that the political parties control not only the U.S. Congress, but all state legislatures as well. We the People are going to have a very difficult time breaking power at the state level in order to get an Article V convention called, but we have no choice but to try. Ethically, we must exhaust all peaceful possibilities before even thinking about taking up arms. The U.S. Constitution, unfortunately, leaves only one peaceful pathway to amend the U.S. Constitution when Congress will not act – an Article V convention called by the vote of two thirds of the states' legislatures.

My advice is that we all begin the practice, at each and every future election, of voting only for candidates for state legislature who promise to introduce and pass a demand for a general constitutional convention under Article V.

THE CONTRACT AND OTHER ANALOGIES

Under the basic law of contract, a document can be "reformed" or changed to match what the parties understood was their agreement when the document has a mistake.[33] Per the Restatement of Contracts:

> "§155. When Mistake of Both Parties as to Written Expression Justifies Reformation
>   Where a writing that evidences or embodies an agreement in whole or in part fails to express the agreement because of a mistake of both

parties as to the contents or effect of the writing, the court may at the request of a party reform the writing to express the agreement . . ."[34]

In The Federalist Number 43, James Madison sold the newly drafted Constitution by describing the Article V Amendment Clause as follows:

"It moreover equally enables the general and state governments to originate the amendment of errors as they may be pointed out by the experience on the one side or on the other."

There is a problem with Madison's statement. Congress can revert into a convention to propose constitutional amendments any time it wishes, upon a simple vote in both chambers. The burden of inertia for thirty-four state legislatures to vote for a constitutional convention is obviously not "equal" to Congress only needing its two chambers to discuss possible constitutional amendments.

There are five key steps to amend the U.S. Constitution through the alternative convention process, but the Constitution fails to expressly provide details for step two regarding how convention delegates are chosen:

1. Two-thirds of state legislatures vote for convention.
2. Convention delegates are elected (by The People, not appointed by state legislatures – this is not stated in Article V, but is deduced from the history, purpose, intent and structure of Article V and the text of other parts of the Constitution.)
3. The Convention forms, prepares rules, makes proposals, debates, deliberates, considers, votes and proposes amendments.
4. Proposals "loop back" through Congress before going to the states; Congress decides whether ratification will be by three-fourths of state legislatures or three-fourths of state ratification conventions.
5. When three-fourths of the states, through whichever mode of ratification is chosen, vote to ratify a proposed amendment, it becomes part of the U.S. Constitution.

Even if thirty-four state legislatures vote for an Article V convention, the convention cannot form or do work until rules are established for which Americans get to attend and vote at the convention. It clearly is not an "equal" process to that utilized when Congress wants to propose an amendment. More importantly, however, is the fact that without a remedy for choosing delegates, we the People have no right or power to a constitutional convention. There is still a condition which must be met, the condition of agreeing to the rules for representation at the convention. It is a conditional promise, which is like no promise at all.[35]

Elections for convention delegates cannot be held until the rules of suffrage are established. The Constitutional Convention Clause within Article V cannot be utilized without some form of legislative agreement as to the rules for the election of delegates. It is literally the one part of the U.S. Constitution that does not follow the Western Legal Tradition, but instead follows the old Soviet Legal Tradition.

In the Soviet Legal Tradition, there was no system of checks and balances and the Doctrine of Separation of Powers was rejected.[36] In the Western Legal Tradition, rights stated in a constitution are considered "active" rights without any need for legislative enactment. In the old Soviet Legal Tradition however, even though the Soviet constitution also included a Bill of Rights similar to ours, a legislative enactment was required before a constitutional right became "active" and could be relied upon or acted upon in the courts.[37] This was part of how the Soviet Communist Party controlled that system.[38]

The Article V Convention Clause may literally be the only clause in our Constitution that follows the old Soviet Legal Tradition by requiring some sort of legislative enactment (beyond the basic two thirds vote of state legislatures for the call of the convention) before We the People can utilize our check and balance of a constitutional convention. This obviously was not the intent of the Framers. The Convention Clause was meant to be a way of amending the Constitution without the consent of the national legislature (especially if the government should become corrupt.) Giving that very legislature the ability to block a check and balance against it obviously does not comport with the intent of our founding document, and the mistake is clearly subject to reformation in order to comply with original intent. Again, if Congress is corrupt or will not act to propose necessary amendments, then the state legislatures must vote for the call of the Article V convention and, to have orderly elections, the step of choosing delegates must be worked out between the People and their state legislatures.

The right of the People to a constitutional convention under Article V is an illusion, what under the law is called an illusory right. Article V deceptively, by false appearances, gives the impression that there is a right of the People to a convention to propose constitutional amendments, when in fact substantively there is no such right until there is general consensus as to a delegate selection process and general voting standards.

Using our right to a constitutional convention can be analogized to moving one's Queen in a game of chess. In chess, the Queen is the most powerful piece because it can move in any direction on the board as far as it can move in that direction. Because of this, chess strategy is to wait to move your Queen so as to protect it from being captured early. The other part of this wisdom is to not wait too long to move your Queen, or it will be too late and you will lose. It is clearly not too early (after nearly 230 years) to call for an Article V convention to address the Constitution's two deep structural defects. The real question is whether we have waited too long.

CHAPTER 5

The Beginning of a Solution – The Tricameralism Amendment

*"In republican government, the legislative authority necessarily predominates. The **remedy** for this inconveniency is to **divide the legislature into different branches**; and to render them, by different modes of election and different principles of action, as little connected with each other as the nature of their common functions and their common dependence on the society will admit. It may even be necessary to guard against dangerous encroachments by still further precautions."*[1]

(JAMES MADISON, THE FEDERALIST NO. 51, FEBRUARY 8, 1788)

AFTER GEORGE WASHINGTON STOOD UP on the last day of the original United States Constitutional Convention, September 17, 1787, and urged the delegates to lower the floor for the amount of people represented by each member of the House from 40,000 persons to 30,000 persons, the convention delegates unanimously voted to make the change. It was literally the last revision to the U.S. Constitution before the Convention delegates voted to approve the document for signing and proposal to the states for ratification.[2] It is also our best expert witness testimony as to what an ideal representation fraction might be.

If we as a nation wanted to return the country to a true democratic republic, with actual meaningful representation at the level contemplated by the people who wrote and ratified the U.S. Constitution, how would we do it? Do we keep adding more and more people to the House of Representatives? It would result in thousands of people sitting in the House. Madison's thoughts at the time were stated in the famous Federalist Number 10, where he discusses a type of Goldilocks Zone for citizen representation in a republic:

"In the first place it is to be remarked that however small the republic may be the representatives must be raised to a certain number in order to guard against the cabals of a few; and that however large it may be they must be limited to a certain number to guard against the confusion of a multitude."[3]

Madison's concerns can be addressed by adding a third division to our legislative branch. Instead of meeting in Washington D.C. in a large assembly, however, the third division would begin its work in small working groups of thirty sub-representatives in each of the 435 Congressional districts. This would be about the same size as the 1787 Convention working group[4], and that size of working group seemed to work fairly well. Just like any other legislative body or convention, committees could be formed where each district sends an emissary to meet with chosen representatives from other districts. Smaller committees could be formed, but the details for such should be worked out by the convention delegates themselves after the call for the convention.

We saw in chapter 2 that in 1920, Congress ended the practice of growing the House of Representatives as the population grew, thereby abandoning the duty to apportion and the duty to guaranty a republican form of government.[5] (See Table 4: *United States Population Increase Over Time Compared to Number of Representatives in U.S. Congress*, at page 20.) For nearly one hundred years, politicians have given almost no thought to how to correct the errors in the U.S. Constitution which have led us to this point, and now population growth and a rapidly changing economic structure are forcing the problem to the forefront.

The inability for one hundred years to address the problem is clearly a failure of the two-party system, and the failure of state legislatures to call for an Article V convention. James Madison, in The Federalist No. 58, makes clear that Congress has a duty to increase congressional representatives as the population increases. Alexander Hamilton confirmed such intent in The Federalist Number 84:

"It is true that this number is intended to be increased; but this is to keep pace with the increase of the population and resources of the country. It is evident, that a lesser number would, even in the first instance, have been unsafe; and that **a continuance of the present number would, in a more advanced stage of population, be a very inadequate representation of the people.**"[6]

Since 1910, there has been no increase in the size of the House of Representatives. Even though human population continues to explode, we still have only 435 representatives in the House of Representatives. Assuming your representative in Congress spends time actually working, and accounting for the fact that the representatives must now spend as much as half of their time collecting free money (campaigning) instead of working, your share of time with your representative is about one second per year. Someone connected has probably already "hogged" your share of time with your so-called "representative."

If increasing the size of the House of Representatives would make that assembly unruly or less effective, there is really only one direction for us to go – to create a third division of the U.S. Congress. As it turns out, by waiting one hundred years and allowing our population size to increase, adding a third division of Congress now makes sense and the cost is justified in order to secure the foundations of our check and balance system.

Members of the House of Representatives now represent nearly 750,000 people. It is not possible to adequately represent the interests of so many. Rather than full representation, members of Congress have no choice but to ration representation because they simply do not have enough time to properly gather their constituents' opinions and grievances. Obviously, our representation system will continue to break down and deteriorate until we perform the task of correcting original error.

The proposed solution is a modern-day version of the originally proposed first amendment which was never ratified, a redesigned Size of Congress Amendment, to reconnect the People to their own representatives in Congress.

The United States Congress is known as a bicameral legislature, referring to the two chambers or divisions of Congress, the House of Representatives and The Senate. If the originally proposed first amendment had come out of conference committee as drafted by either the House or Senate, requiring an additional representative be added for every growth of 50,000 to 60,000 people, it would require over five-thousand members in the House of Representatives. An assembly of that size would likely become unruly and difficult to manage. So, what do we do to return voters to a level of approximately 30,000 people per representative, leaving room for future population growth? We create a third division of Congress, which "We the people" then leverage as a check and balance against out of control government in each of the three branches of the national government.

The proposed amendment to add a third division to Congress with check and balance powers is not some radical alteration of the Constitution, but an "add-on" or "build-on" to its existing structure to account for our substantial population increase since our nation's founding. The idea came out of one of the best known of The Federalist Papers, a series of articles written by James Madison, Alexander Hamilton and John Jay to convince the American people to approve the "new" Constitution. In The Federalist Number 51, Madison teaches the concept of a check and balance system. With respect to the legislative branch:

In republican government, <u>the legislative authority necessarily</u> <u>predominates. The **remedy** for this inconveniency is to **divide the**</u>

<u>legislature into different branches</u>; and to render them, by different modes of election and different principles of action, as little connected with each other as the nature of their common functions and their common dependence on the society will admit. <u>It may even be necessary to guard against dangerous encroachments by still further precautions.</u>[7]

Most scholars look at the last sentence of that passage as a reference to adding a Bill of Rights, because that <u>was</u> the big issue between the drafting of the Constitution and state ratification. However, with a fresh set of eyes and keen awareness of continuing rapid human population growth, another possibility comes to light. Divide the legislature into three branches, assigning the checks and balances needed **as learned through experience.**

Structural reforms are clearly needed in our Constitutional system to reestablish Congressional responsiveness to public opinion. As set forth in prior chapters, there are two primary structural defects, **learned through experience**, in the U.S. Constitution: 1) The failure to complete the Bill of Rights to ensure adequate representation strength, including meaningful access to one's representative, and 2) the failure of Article V to provide any rules or procedures for a constitutional convention, including the absence of any express standards for choosing the voting delegates at any such convention.

In place of the Size of Congress Amendment, I propose an updated amendment of dynamic design which I call the Tricameralism Amendment.[8] Rather than two chambers of Congress, we will move to a system with three divisions of Congress, giving particular check and balance powers to the third division designed to rebuild the foundations of our representative system and reconnect the citizens to our own government. The third body of Congress will give each citizen access to a sub-representative at about the representation strength enjoyed by the founding generation, one representative per 30,000 people.[9]

To justify the cost of an increase in the size of Congress, the third level will need to have some form of Constitutional power to be able to clean up corruption in the system, including influence over the other two houses of Congress as well as over the executive and judicial branches. Interestingly, Alexander Hamilton predicted, in The Federalist Number 84, that serious amendments needed would take the form of a structural change or addition:

> "For my own part, I acknowledge a thorough conviction that any amendments which may, upon mature consideration, be thought useful, will be applicable to the organization of government, not to the mass of its powers . . ."[10]

George Washington, in his inaugural address, provided these insights to guide the formulation of future amendments to the U.S. Constitution:

> "Besides the ordinary objects submitted to your care, it will remain with your judgment to decide, how far an exercise of the occasional power delegated by the Fifth article of the Constitution is rendered expedient at the present juncture by the nature of objections which have been urged against the System, or by the degree of inquietude which has given birth to them. Instead of undertaking particular recommendations on this subject, in which I could be guided by no lights derived from official opportunities, I shall again give way to my entire confidence in your discernment and pursuit of the public good: For I assure myself that whilst you <u>carefully avoid every alteration which might endanger the benefits of an United and effective Government, or which ought to await the **future lessons of experience**; a reverence for the characteristic rights of freemen, and a regard for the public harmony, will sufficiently influence your deliberations on the question how far the former can be more impregnably fortified, or the latter be safely and advantageously promoted</u>."[11]

With these matters in mind, and after much thought and deliberation, I propose that a third division of Congress be formed pursuant to constitutional amendment, comprised of thirty sub-representatives in each of our 435 Congressional districts. Initially, I am calling the proposed third division of Congress the Constitutional Enclaves, signifying their role in maintaining a properly working check and balance system. The Constitutional Enclaves would be delegated the following three powers:

1. Power to Remove and Replace Representative in House of Representatives

First, in the third division (the Constitutional Enclaves,) which will consist of 30 sub-representatives in each of the 435 Congressional districts, the thirty sub-representatives in each district will be able to replace that district's representative in the House of Representatives with one of that district's 30 sub-representatives, upon a 2/3 vote (20 out of 30.)

Forget term limits, this is far better. For example, if a representative's allegiance appears to be to wealthy campaign donors rather than to the people in his or her district, you would be able to push the thirty sub-representatives in your district to remove that representative and replace her or him with one of the thirty sub-representatives whose priorities are better aligned with the people in your district.

Moreover, this change would modify Article 1, section 2, paragraph 4 of the Constitution, which currently requires state governors to call a special election to fill vacancies in Congress. The current Constitutional rule can allow an entire district to go without representation in Congress for months, and those may be months when some of the most crucial matters come up for vote (think declarations of war, proposals for Constitutional amendments, and big legislation like "Obamacare".) Likewise, if Congress will not act when a large consensus of the citizens want action, a movement can begin to remove and replace your representative with a sub-representative prepared to do the People's business.

The rule allowing replacement of a representative with one of the 30 sub-representatives of that district will allow all districts to avoid periods of taxation without representation as is experienced under the current rule. The three-quarters of a million people in each district would not then have to suffer for the "knuckle headed" behavior of their representative. Recent examples of this injustice are representatives who resign after they are caught in marital infidelity, using cocaine, or committing tax fraud or other crimes of deception. The 30 sub-representatives would vote for one of their thirty to go to Washington, D.C. and immediately take over the seat of the representative for that district.

This additional structure built onto the existing structure would be better than term limits because your district could replace poor performers but would not be forced by term limits to lose decent leaders.

2. Power to Make Legislative Rules

Second, we take away from the Senate and from the House of Representatives the power to exclusively make their own rules, and instead delegate that primary power to the third division of Congress.

We generally expect the rules to be a way to keep the peace in Congress. We do not expect the rule-making process to be used as a weapon of one party against another. People get angry when rules are broken, but people can become absolutely livid if the rules are changed "in the middle of the game," not by a neutral party, but by the other "team." The change would finally eliminate one of the worst conflicts of interest created by the Constitution, allowing Congress to make its own rules.

It would remind Congresspersons who their actual employers are, We the People, not themselves and not the ultra-rich who finance their campaigns and lifestyles. The change will promote a legislature that works for the benefit of the entire country rather than a Congress which behaves like two large law firms so focused on winning that they have forgotten that We the People are their clients.

3. Power to Propose Constitutional Amendments for Consideration by the States

Third, and perhaps the most important power of all to justify the third level's existence and cost, is to give the third level the power to propose constitutional amendments to the states for ratification if 3/4 of the states (38 out of 50) approve the proposed amendment.

As it turns out, our Constitution has a real and meaningful flaw. It does not set out any of the rules and procedures for a constitutional convention under Article V. There is no guidance as to how many delegates will attend, what percentage vote is required to send a proposed amendment from a constitutional convention to the states, or any other rule or procedure necessary for the convention.

The current Constitution is silent as to the rules and procedures for a constitutional convention, and we as a nation are now **informed by experience** of the need to amend the amendment clause of the Constitution, Article V, in order to clear up the procedure for future constitutional conventions. The constitutional convention was meant to be a check and balance to be used at times when the government is corrupt or no longer has sufficient connection to the electorate to be responsive to the People. It is our peaceful, legal check and balance, but if you do not use it, it is like not having a check and balance at all.

If the American people are finally serious about standing up and taking back the reins of our own country, we must begin to use our check and balance of an Article V convention. The third division of Congress will allow us to replace a representative at once, which I assure you will reestablish some responsiveness out of the House of Representatives. Most of the representatives in Congress are now rich and connected, but the loss of salary and prestige will still act as a psychological deterrent to poor congressional behavior. If the American people were to adopt The Tricameralism Amendment, it would be a major improvement, assuming the American people are active as to their rights and interests within our governing system.

The third division of Congress, at least until it agrees to new rules for the size and composition of an Article V convention, can act as the pre-convention and take on what might be a protracted fight over the rules of the Convention. In the meantime, we can go ahead and give it the power to make suggestions for amendments like a Convention would, and we could get some of the most pressing changes accomplished, presupposing sufficient agreement at the state legislative level for such changes.

So, in review, the third level, which might be called the "Constitutional Enclaves" to describe their role in Constitutional balancing, will have three powers:

1. The power to replace a district representative with one of the thirty sub-representatives in each district, on 2/3 vote of the thirty sub-representatives in that district;
2. The power to make rules for the House and Senate;
3. The power to propose Constitutional amendments to the state legislatures or state ratification conventions.

This proposal meets George Washington's guidelines for amendment set forth in his inaugural address. It does not endanger the benefits of a united and effective government because we no longer have a united and effective government. The proposal would reopen the path to a better government by reestablishing the foundations of our check and balance system. The second factor, awaiting the future lessons of experience, is the core concept of this book. We have awaited the lessons of experience for too long. Now that experience has taught us where the defects are, we must act.

The proposal promotes reverence for the rights of free men by allowing more men <u>and</u> women into the governing process and giving more than 535 people a legislative voice in a nation approaching a third of a billion people. The fourth factor, public harmony, has been suffering for the past thirty years. The proposal seeks to rebuild trust between the American people and reestablish public harmony.

Initial draft language of one version of a tricameralism amendment follows. A basic organizational chart accompanies the draft amendment at Illustration 2: *Tricameralism.*

Illustration 2: **Tricameralism**, Simple Organizational Chart

(Emphasis on Legislative Branch)

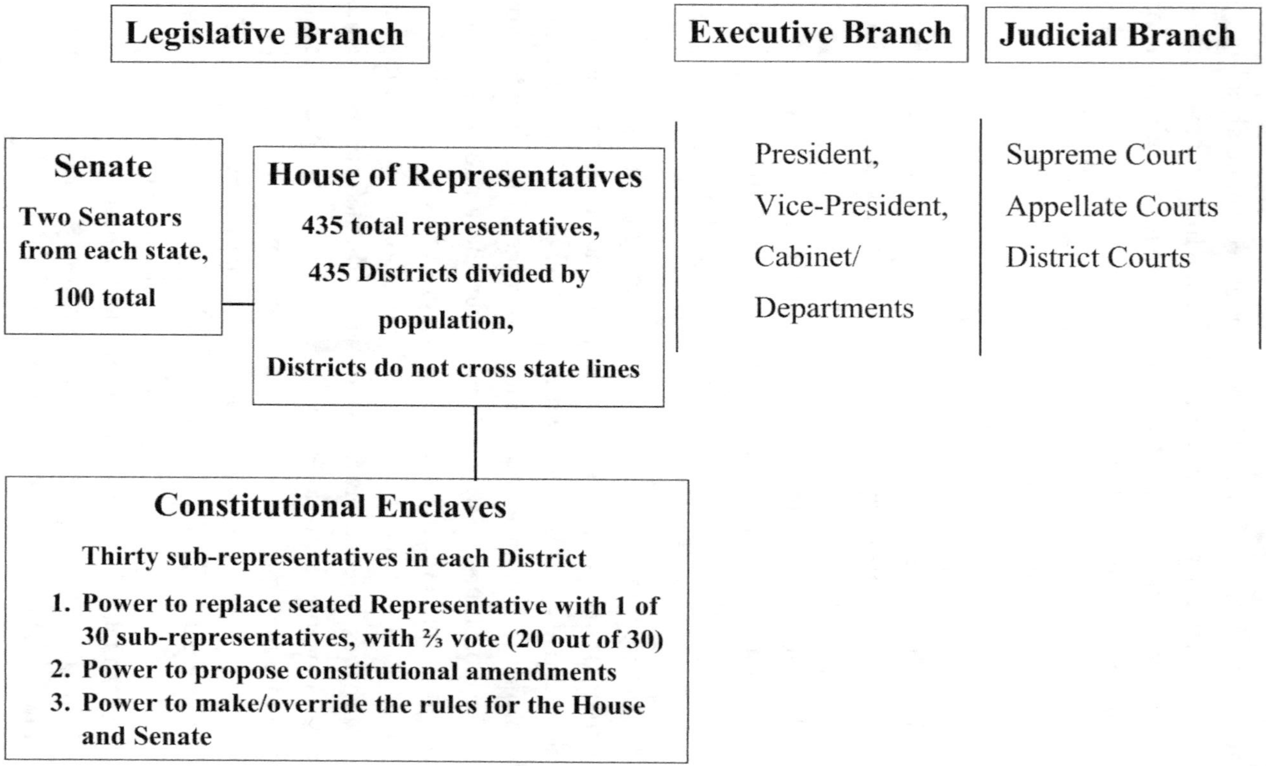

Legislative Branch	Executive Branch	Judicial Branch

Executive Branch

President,
Vice-President,
Cabinet/
Departments

Judicial Branch

Supreme Court
Appellate Courts
District Courts

House of Representatives

435 total representatives,

435 Districts divided by
population,

Districts do not cross state lines

Senate

Two Senators
from each state,

100 total

Constitutional Enclaves

Thirty sub-representatives in each District

1. Power to replace seated Representative with 1 of
30 sub-representatives, with ⅔ vote (20 out of 30)
2. Power to propose constitutional amendments
3. Power to make/override the rules for the House
and Senate

THE TRICAMERALISM AMENDMENT – DRAFT LANGUAGE

All legislative Powers herein granted shall be vested in a Congress of the United States, which shall consist of a Senate, a House of Representatives and a third division of Congress consisting of a body of subdistrict representatives in each Congressional District, known as the Constitutional Enclaves. Each Congressional District shall have a Constitutional Enclave, consisting of 30 subdistrict representatives. (Modifies United States Constitution, Article 1, Section 1, and other sections)

No political party affiliation will be required to serve as a subdistrict representative, and no party affiliation will be placed upon election ballots in relation to the election of subdistrict representatives.

Each subdistrict representative must be a resident of the state in which that representative is elected, must be at least 20 years old, and must have been a Citizen and resident of the United States for at least 10 years.

Each Constitutional Enclave will consist of 30 members elected by the citizens from 30 subdistricts within each Congressional District, drawn to resemble rough diamond shapes by a computer program. The Enclaves will not be housed in the nation's Capital, but in their own districts using existing buildings owned by the federal government or provided without charge by their state or other government or charitable entities.

Initial salaries of subdistrict representatives will be $37,500 per year, and shall thereafter be set by national vote of the electorate in years of Presidential elections.

The Constitutional Enclaves (the third body or third division of Congress) shall have the following powers:

POWER TO REPLACE REPRESENTATIVE

1. Each Constitutional Enclave will have the power, upon two thirds vote of such enclave, to replace its district's representative in the House of Representatives with one of the Constitutional Enclave's 30 members.

{Shorthand: 20 of 30 subdistrict representatives can replace that district's representative with one of the 30 members of that Enclave.}

POWER TO PROPOSE CONSTITUTIONAL AMENDMENTS

2. The Constitutional Enclaves have the power to review potentially beneficial constitutional changes and propose constitutional amendments, which shall be valid to all Intents and Purposes, as Part of this Constitution, when ratified by the Legislatures of three fourths of the several States, or by Conventions in three fourths thereof, as the one or the other Mode of Ratification may be proposed by the Congress. For an amendment to qualify for presentation to the states for ratification, the amendment must be approved for such purpose by a 60% vote by at least 55% of the Enclaves. (Modifies Article V of the U.S. Constitution.)

{Shorthand: The Constitutional Enclaves have the power to propose Constitutional amendments to the States, in addition to Congress. The Constitutional Enclaves will act as the Article V Convention, until the Enclaves comes up with a better format for the Convention. We secure principles of representation first, then focus on process.}

[Note: This power can be limited, for example, for a ten or twenty-year period while the Constitutional Enclaves set up the procedural architecture for a United States Constitutional Convention, or we can agree to simply choose The Tricameral System to serve as our Constitutional Convention. In addition to other checks and balances in the Constitution, people tend to forget that the upper two houses of Congress also have the right to propose amendments to the states. If people become concerned that the Constitutional Enclaves have too much power, the upper two houses can offer amendments to the state legislatures to limit and "check and balance" the Enclaves.]

RULE MAKING POWER

3. The Constitutional Enclaves, collectively upon 60% of the Enclaves passing by 60% vote within each Enclave, have the power to change or make the rules of both the Senate and the House of Representatives. In all cases where a rule of the Senate or the House of Representatives is inconsistent

with any rule provided by the Constitutional Enclaves, the rule provided by the Constitutional Enclaves will prevail. The Constitutional Enclaves, collectively by majority vote of a majority of the Enclaves, shall be the sole judge of whether a Senate or House rule conflicts with a rule provided by the Constitutional Enclaves. (Modifies Article I, §5, ¶2)

The Constitutional Enclaves, as a third body of Congress, collectively may make its own rules and the rules of the individual enclaves. Each individual enclave may make its own rules to the extent not inconsistent with rules made by the enclaves collectively. The Constitutional Enclaves collectively by majority vote of a majority of the enclaves, shall be the sole judge of whether a rule of an individual enclave conflicts with a rule provided by the Constitutional Enclaves collectively.

{Shorthand: The Constitutional Enclaves can force a rule change in either the House or Senate, but makes its own rules as a collective body.}

Alternative addition #1: Each enclave's power to replace that district's representative cannot be exercised during the first six months of each representative's term.

Alternative addition #2: Each enclave's power to replace that district's representative cannot be exercised during the first year of any representative serving their first term as a United States Representative.

Alternative addition #3: After the selection of the 30 subdistrict representatives, the five highest vote recipients who were not selected as one of the 30 subdistrict representatives shall be retained as alternate subdistrict representatives in the event any of the original 30 members is not able to serve to the end of the next term.

Alternative addition #4: If any subdistrict representative is unable to serve to the end of term, the next highest vote recipient in that subdistrict will serve as alternate subdistrict representative.

Alternative addition #5: Each Constitutional Enclave will consist of 30 members elected from 15 subdistricts, drawn to resemble rough diamond shapes by a computer program, with one man and one woman member from each subdistrict. [Note: With this alternative, some election costs will be cut in half because the number of subdistricts are cut in half.]

CHAPTER 6

Flexibility of a Tricameral Legislative System

"It was much to be desired that the objections to the plan recommended might be made as few as possible. **The smallness of the proportion of Representatives had been considered by many members of the Convention, an insufficient security for the rights & interests of the people.** *He acknowledged that it had always appeared to himself among the exceptionable parts of the plan; and late as the present moment was for admitting amendments, he thought this of so much consequence that it would give much satisfaction to see it adopted."*[1]

(James Madison's notes of 1787 Constitutional
Convention, paraphrasing George Washington,
September 17, 1787, signing day.)

A Tricameral Legislative System would be flexible and serviceable. It would give us the freedom to do more with our governing system. We could use it for a number of different purposes. If the Constitutional Enclaves (or Article V convention if in another format) and the state legislatures should agree in sufficient Constitutional numbers, the system could be used as follows:

1. **Power Rebalancing:** The Constitutional Enclaves can slowly and methodically examine ways to shift powers from the federal government

back to the states and People. Many people do not realize that today's Constitution is not interpreted in the same manner as just after ratification in 1787.

After the Great Depression began, President Roosevelt urged the U.S. Congress to pass "New Deal" legislation to allow a social safety net and regulation of working conditions. Each piece of legislation was challenged and the U.S. Supreme Court kept declaring the legislation unconstitutional.[2]

President Roosevelt finally lost his patience and threatened to "pack the court." His plan was to get Congress to add six more justices to the Supreme Court, for a total of fifteen. With the larger court, President Roosevelt would have enough votes on the Supreme Court to have the majority needed to declare New Deal legislation constitutional. By doing so, he challenged the intended check and balance structure of the federal government by threatening to overturn Supreme Court rulings by rapidly increasing the amount of "liberal" justices on the Court.

The sitting Supreme Court backed down. In 1936, the Court invalidated, on a 5 to 4 vote, a New York minimum wage law in the case of *Morehead v. New York ex rel. Tipaldo*.[3] Just one year later, Justice Owen Roberts changed his ideological mind and voted in favor of Washington's minimum wage law in the case of *West Coast Hotel v. Parrish*[4], which put the Court at 5 to 4 in favor of constitutionality. According to historian David M. Kennedy:

The decision in *Parrish* amounted to "the greatest constitutional somersault in history," declared one commentator. "On Easter Sunday," said another, "state minimum wage laws were unconstitutional, but about noon on Easter Monday, these laws were constitutional." **The key to this reversal was the shift of a single vote**. Justice Roberts had sided with the conservative quartet in *Tipaldo*, but now he followed Hughes and joined the liberal trio . . . . "By nodding his head instead of shaking it," an observer noted, Owen Roberts, one single human being, had amended the

Constitution of the United States." Pundits immediately called Roberts' judicial pirouette "the switch in time that saved nine," a deft maneuver that spiked Roosevelt's Court reform while ushering in a new jurisprudential regime.[5]

The U.S. Constitution is intended to delegate only limited powers to the national government, as emphasized by the Ninth and Tenth Amendments. Article I, Section 8 of the Constitution lists 18 paragraphs of powers delegated to the national government. The third paragraph of such section grants the United States the power to regulate commerce among the states, and is known as the Commerce Clause. For one-hundred fifty years, the Commerce Clause was understood to make a distinction between interstate commerce and intrastate commerce. If economic activity took place solely within the borders of an individual state, it was considered intrastate commerce and the U.S. Congress had no power to regulate such activity.

While the *Parrish* case dealt with state legislation, it heralded in a change to the Court's view on the constitutionality of national legislation as well. For fifty years after the *Parrish* case, the Court upheld the constitutionality of state and national socioeconomic legislation.[6] The shift was based upon what lawyers call the "Dormant Commerce Clause." When the Supreme Court made its shift in ideology to allow the Commerce Clause to be reinterpreted, it is said that the clause had been dormant, and the Supreme Court had simply decided after decades to wake it up to allow regulation of anything that could have an effect on interstate commerce.

Historically, the Commerce Clause was not understood to give the national government so much power. It was a radical change in American constitutional law. An example of what some say is a legitimate criticism of the Dormant Commerce Clause is a Supreme Court case, *Wickard v. Filburn*[7], that ruled that the federal government could prohibit people from growing wheat on their own property for personal use because private home farming would have an "economic effect" on interstate commerce by lowering the market price and harming commercial farmers.

Historically, if such was the understanding at the time the Constitution was written, the Constitution would never have been ratified.

The Dormant Commerce Clause could be seen as an over correction, and with the passage of time we are now seeing damaging effects from the court's decision. People with this view would probably want the opportunity to discuss the possibility of returning to the states and/or The People some of the expanded powers of the federal government as a result of the Dormant Commerce Clause rulings. For example, to preserve good will among the nation's inhabitants, some might argue that certain topics should be handled by the states thus countering the earlier over correction of opening up the Dormant Commerce Clause.

Instead of attempting to unravel eighty years of case law, delegates to an Article V convention could look for compromises which preserve our social safety net while strengthening the check and balance features of federalism and strengthening individual rights to use one's property at its highest valued usage. Using a type of "line item" approach, carving out areas of commerce reserved to the states for regulation or prohibiting certain types of regulation, might work best.

2. **Individual Right to Keep and Bear Arms**: There have been terrible tragedies in our nation involving the use of firearms, including what is basically the mass murder of school children and other Americans. There are tremendous motivations to curb gun use as a result.

Of all the nations on this planet, only the United States, Mexico and Guatemala have a constitutional right to bear arms.[8] Nonetheless, the United States has generally been one of the more stable nations, and some will argue that the Second Amendment Right to Keep and Bear Arms has helped such stability. Moreover, if one studies the history of the continent of Africa, both during the colonial period and the period immediately after, those communities which did not have access to modern arms, if not decimated by groups with European arms, have been and were economically oppressed and unable to develop. If the American working class does not have access to arms, chances are that over time such would result in the further erosion of the economic and ultimate freedom of the American worker.

Despite the horrific murders which continue to take place, I still would highly advise the American working class never to give up its access to arms. It acts as a check and balance in our structural system[9], and helps to act as a check and balance between workers and the wealthy.

Amazingly, the first Supreme Court case to ever deal with the issue was in 2008, 219 years after the Bill of Rights was written, in the case of *District of Columbia v. Heller*.[10] Many Americans do not realize that the Supreme Court, until 2008, never acknowledged an individual right to keep and bear arms for self-defense.

The language of the Second Amendment is not crystal clear: "A well regulated Militia, being necessary to the security of a free State, the right of the people to keep and bear Arms, shall not be infringed."[11] Lawyers could interpret this as an individual right to keep and bear arms, for self defense. They could also interpret it as meaning that the right to keep and bear arms is only held by those in a regulated militia.

Washington, D.C. had a statute generally prohibiting the possession of handguns. The statute was challenged by Richard Heller, a police officer who wanted to keep a handgun at home.

The Supreme Court split in a 5 to 4 vote. Recently deceased Justice Antonin Scalia wrote the majority opinion. The so-called conservative wing held that "the District's ban on handgun possession in the home violates the Second Amendment, as does its prohibition against rendering any lawful firearm in the home operable for the purpose of immediate self-defense."[12] The holding found, "on the basis of both text and history, that the Second Amendment conferred an individual right to keep and bear arms."[13]

However, **with just a single changed vote** by the members of the Supreme Court on the issue, our government may acquire, through Supreme Court ruling, the power to basically take guns away from the citizenry. The liberal wing of the Court had a radically different perspective, and stated that the Second Amendment "protects the right to keep and bear arms for certain military purposes, but that it does not curtail the Legislature's power to regulate the nonmilitary use and ownership of weapons. . ."[14] Justice Stevens' dissenting opinion made clear the viewpoint of the liberal wing that "the [Second] Amendment should not be interpreted as limiting the authority of Congress to regulate the use or possession of firearms for purely civilian purposes."[15]

In the discussion at the beginning of this chapter regarding the Dormant Commerce Clause, we learned that **just one Supreme Court justice changing his or her viewpoint** could lead to what is effectively a constitutional amendment by the Court. It is no mistake that the very next topic to discuss is the Second Amendment, because we are one Supreme Court Justice's biased viewpoint away from writing the Second Amendment out of the Constitution as a protector of civilian gun ownership rights. The man who wrote the opinion, Justice Antonin Scalia, is now dead and the two political parties "argued over his corpse" about who should replace him. Republican senators successfully refused to give President Obama's choice of replacement, Merrick Garland, a hearing or vote, hoping that a Republican will win the Presidency in 2016. If a Democrat had become the next President, chances are the balance on the Supreme Court with regard to the Second Amendment would have shifted and the *Heller* case could quickly get overruled by the liberal wing of the Court.

If the *Heller* case should get overturned, the only way to reestablish the individual right to keep and bear arms, even if not in an "organized militia," is to amend the Constitution to make clear that individuals have such a right. If Congress will not act to make such amendment, then the only other avenue to amendment is to call for an Article V convention.

From a practical perspective, it seems that an individual right to bear arms is most consistent with our collective interest in "the security of a free state." Upon invasion, all able bodied can pick up arms and take up a position in defense of family and country. If the contrary rule were chosen, groups of terrorists could kill at will and create the sort of terror that eliminates any true concept of liberty in our land.

That being said, it is also a matter of the interests and liberties of Americans to not be killed in cold blood by one of our fellow Americans with a gun. If gun safety could be had without burdening interests in freedom and security, then we should pursue such safety measures. In the current political climate, where some days it seems that the leadership of the two political parties cannot even behave like adults, the best chance of reconciling the various interests involved would be in an Article V convention (assuming the citizens are sophisticated enough to vote for more calm and scholarly representatives to the Article V convention, rather than some of the bullying personalities in Congress now.)

Once again, we have no system in place for electing delegates to an Article V convention. If the *Heller* case should get overturned, and Congress does not act, we will be left without the ability to begin a convention and the citizenry will likely soon be at the mercy of invasion, terrorism and a powerfully armed government and law enforcement apparatus.

3. **Set the salaries of the House and Senate:** It is a clear conflict of interest to give Congress the power to set its own salary[16] (if only we all had such ability.) We could eliminate this conflict of interest by transferring such power to the Constitutional Enclaves, and allow the Enclaves to set the upper two chambers' salary.

4. **Eliminate gerrymandering:** Over the course of time, the political party practice of gerrymandering districts has made our system far less competitive and far less democratic. The practice favors incumbents and shuts out all but those willing to swear loyalty to one of the two political parties (rather than the people each representative actually represents.) The Constitutional Enclaves could be given the power to draw legislative districts under rules prohibiting gerrymandering and setting forth a more neutral procedure for how districts are drawn. This would eliminate the current practice of collusion of the two political parties, which draw the districts to favor party interests.

This proposal is unique in the sense that it arguably would take power from the states and transfer it to the national government. However, in practice the change would probably best be seen as transferring power from the political parties, which are dominated by the national arms of the two major parties, and placing power closer to the People.

5. **Documenting and categorizing citizen concerns:** Because each member of the House of Representatives now represents nearly 750,000 people rather than the 30,000 the text of the Constitution anticipated[17], our share of time with our so-called "representative" is around one second per year. The Enclaves could serve as the main conduit for the public to communicate its viewpoints on ongoing legislation. Citizens would communicate with their sub-representative. Sub-representatives would tally such citizen communications and provide such information to their Representative in the House. This would allow the governing system to come up with solutions before the complaints ramp up too high. We could even develop an internet survey system to get the public's opinion before votes in the House of Representatives.

6. **Address campaign finance.** Many Americans are not aware that in 2010 the Supreme Court overruled the majority will of both Congress and the People with regard to limits on campaign finance. In the case of *Citizens United v. Federal Election Commission*[18], the conservative wing of the Court struck down legislation limiting money in politics and instead unbalanced our system of inequality further by allowing unlimited amounts of money to be spent in elections. The citizens, if fully aware, might be able to get Congress to propose a constitutional amendment to address campaign finance, but enough politicians have decided to take advantage of the new imbalance which favors the rich that nothing has been done.

The *Citizens United* case reflects a type of snobbish aristocratic bias of our judicial branch. If you have working class bias, the following sentence from the Court's opinion is perhaps one of the dumbest sentences ever written by a Supreme Court justice:

> "The appearance of influence or access, furthermore, will not cause the electorate to lose faith in our democracy."[19]

What the nobility on the Supreme Court do not seem to understand is that, except for those who benefit from system imbalance, **the American people by and large have already lost faith in our democracy.**[20]

According to the New York Times: 84% of Americans think that money has too much influence in American politics; 46% think we need to completely rebuild our campaign system, while another 39% (for a total of 87%) think fundamental changes are needed; 78% agree that even groups not affiliated with a candidate should be limited in the amount of money spent on political campaigns; 77% want limits on the amount of money individuals can donate to campaigns; and 75% agree that groups not affiliated with a candidate should be required to publicly disclose their contributors.[21]

When each voter has to share a representative with 740,000 people rather than the 30,000 figure sold to the 1788-89 American voter, and the Court now sanctions a pay for access system, it actually works to cut off access to not only the vast majority of workers (including "want to be" workers,) it also cuts off access to small businesses as well.

The *Citizens United* ruling literally decided in such a way as to obtain the opposite effect of the Court's goal. The Court stated "[d]emocracy is premised on responsiveness." The ruling basically handed a gift of politician responsiveness to the wealthy while cutting off American workers, youth and independents from the governing process. In light of the fact that the system has not been maintained and there has been no constitutional adjustment to account for rapid human population growth after 1800, the Court's ruling in *Citizens United* **effectively cuts off congressional responsiveness to public opinion unless you are rich.**

7. Shift decision-making responsibilities of entire administrative agencies to the Constitutional Enclaves, eliminating costs by streamlining: This would shift power away from the Executive Branch by allowing the electorate to vote for these decision-makers rather than giving the power to choose such decision-makers to the President and his party. Once the decision-makers are elected by the People, we would have more control over the entire decision-making process relating to regulations as well as expense.

8. Leadership Incubator: The current two party political system in America gives a false impression that we have a choice. In the former Soviet Union, one political party (the Communist Party) chose who would be on the ballot and voters had only one "choice." In America's two party system, the two political parties choose who will be on the ballot and the People choose from two poor choices. The illusion that we have a choice in a two-party system may actually be more dangerous to our long-term liberties than a one-party system.

In the current system, the People really have no way of judging the honesty and integrity of the candidates pre-chosen by the political parties. If we were to adopt a tricameral legislative system, the People would be able to "eyeball" their sub-representatives, not just the one they voted for, but the twenty-nine other sub-representatives as well. The District now has the option of looking to the third division of Congress as a type of "farm system" for leadership, which also acts as a check and balance against the power of the political parties.

9. Override a Representative's vote: We could give the third level of Congress the ability to override a vote of that district's representative in the House of Representatives. For example, many Americans were vehemently opposed to the Affordable Care Act ("Obamacare.") If we set up the system properly, the 30 district sub-representatives could override a vote for or against legislation with perhaps a 60% vote of the 30 Enclave members. We could also limit this power, for example, to three times per year, akin to a football coach's limit of throwing red flags to challenge a referee's call. Perhaps the override voting power should not be allowed, however, for exigent national security matters, such as declarations of war, so language would have to be developed to address such issues.

10. Confirm and/or choose Supreme Court Justices: One of the most important principles in our Constitutional system is The Rule of Law. The current U.S. Supreme Court is beginning to be seen as little more than a political body, with more and more rulings ignoring the principle of *stare decisis*. This development is extremely dangerous to our system. *Stare decisis* is the principle that the interpretation of the laws should remain constant, not bounce around with the political winds. When the interpretation of the laws is consistent over time, the People have more veneration for the laws and behavior is better all around.

If people do not see the laws as legitimate, but as part of the same system of alternating party dominance and alternating political acts of revenge which a two-party Congress promotes[22], we run the risk of the electorate simply ignoring the law. Per George Washington in his farewell address:

> The alternate domination of one faction over another, sharpened by the spirit of revenge natural to party dissension, which in different ages and countries has perpetrated the most horrid enormities, is itself a frightful despotism. But this leads at length to a more formal and permanent despotism. The disorders and miseries which result gradually incline the minds of men to seek security and repose in the absolute power of an individual; and sooner or later the chief of some prevailing faction, more able or more fortunate than his competitors, turns this disposition to the purposes of his own elevation on the ruins of public liberty.[23]

We could give the Constitutional Enclaves an equal ability to the Senate to confirm Supreme Court Justices (and even other judges and officials.) Future Presidents could choose to try to confirm by either route. Over time, this should result in more "middle of the road" judges and reduce acrimony in the upper two chambers.

We could even take away from the President the right to choose Supreme Court Justices, and transfer that power to The Constitutional Enclaves. The Enclaves could even set up some sort of electoral system within the Enclaves to vote from a choice of Justices. This would help to eliminate some of the Executive Branch's power and return power more directly to The People.

11. **Difficult Legislation:** It is possible to set up the system to allow The Constitutional Enclaves to deal with difficult legislative topics which Congress has refused to address (for example, problems with healthcare, Medicare, Social Security, The War Powers Act, and the rapid development of new technologies without meaningful effort by Congress to protect Americans' privacy and other rights.) Congress has too many responsibilities to perform when you look at it from the perspective that only 535 people are handling the business of a nation of almost one-third of a billion humans. We could start by giving the Enclaves one issue, for example Social Security, and let the Enclaves work on the problem more slowly and methodically without all of the political circus of the upper two chambers.

12. **Addressing the threat of secretive "think tanks":** Americans are accustomed to the concept that public legislation will be discussed in public. The wealthy have found a way around this great American tradition. They bankroll "think tanks" with capitalist profit-minded people who write pre-packaged legislation and then have legislators introduce the legislation in a type of blitzkrieg political strategy. This catches opposition parties off guard and avoids a full and complete public airing of the advantages and disadvantages of proposed legislation. It goes against the tradition of the Senate of thoroughly vetting all issues and is a potentially dangerous development to our interests and liberty. The Constitutional Enclaves could act as a check and balance to this behavior by acting as the voters' think tanks and defending against such guerilla legislative tactics.

13. **Internet voting "research and development":** Because the proposed third division of Congress does not actually vote in the legislative process of the upper two houses, and leaves the basic traditional legislative process untouched with all its check and balance powers against the other two branches of government intact, it has some freedom to experiment in areas that Congress is not willing to do. For example, the Enclaves can experiment with an internet voting system, to get people's opinions on legislation rather than rely upon commercial profit-minded polling companies. Over time, we should be able to work out the "bugs" of the system so it can be used in general elections as well.

14. **End Games with the Judicial Branch Budget.** One of the most damaging factors to our check and balance system is when one branch of government crosses over check and balance lines into the jurisdiction of another branch. One way that the legislative branch damages the judicial branch and the check and balance system as a whole is by not providing the courts with a sufficient budget to properly handle their caseloads. For the past twenty years, this has been the regular practice of Congress.

Again, per George Washington as his Farewell Address:

> It is important, likewise, that the habits of thinking in a free country should inspire caution in those entrusted with its administration to confine themselves within their respective constitutional spheres, avoiding in the exercise of the powers of one department to encroach upon another. **The spirit of encroachment tends to consolidate the powers of all the departments in one and thus to create, whatever the form of government, a real despotism**. A just estimate of that love of power and proneness to abuse it which predominates in the human heart is sufficient to satisfy us of the truth of this position . . . . If in the opinion of the people the distribution or modification of the constitutional powers be in any particular wrong, let it be corrected by an amendment in

the way which the Constitution designates. But **let there be no change by usurpation**; for though this, in one instance, may be the instrument of good, **it is the customary weapon by which free governments are destroyed.**[24]

In light of such considerations, it would be completely appropriate for an Article V convention to consider some constitutional mechanism to ensure that the judicial branch has a sufficient budget for the judges and staff that it needs to perform its function to keep the peace. When the legislative branch does not properly fund the judicial branch, it enhances further the power of the wealthy. The rich and the teams of lawyers which only the rich (including corporations) can afford are then able to manipulate defects in the system to lead to further imbalance, unfairness in the system and wealth inequality.

15. **Return Democracy to the Committee Process:** The proposed third division of Congress, through its rule-making power, could push the committee process in the upper two chambers of Congress toward a more democratic process. One big problem is the way experts are chosen. Desired opinions are "shopped" for, and once the politicians and lawyers find the expert opinion they want, that is when they "buy" the opinion they have been shopping for and hire that expert.

Since the American people are paying for the expert, and over 40% of American voters are now independents without a representative in Congress[25], 40% of Americans pay for two sets of experts without any benefit. Instead, they are paying for a "pissing contest" between the two "great" political parties. It is taxation without representation at its most corrupt. The Constitutional Enclaves could protect the People's pocketbook by requiring tax dollars to support a more accurate and beneficial process to all. This also serves as a type of check and balance between the People and the two political parties.

16. **Land Use Issues:** Recently we have seen an increase in militia activity and challenges to the national government holding on to large amounts of land which is restricted in use. These issues are long-standing and unresolved. Without taking sides, I would simply suggest that with a third division in Congress, these groups first of all would at least get some access to the legislative process through the Constitutional Enclaves. Second, those making the challenge seem more frustrated than violent, and the Enclaves could give the issue the concentrated study which it deserves in order to prevent social unrest and violence, which I believe the parties involved all wish for as well.

17. **As National Security requires more surveillance, increase privacy and other protections:** Our Constitution did not contemplate endless warfare with non-nations and terrorists. During what I call "War Time Constitution" (contrasted with "Peace Time Constitution,") the entire Bill of Rights is weakened. For example, the Supreme Court case that found it constitutional to place Japanese-Americans in internment camps during World War II, *Korematsu v. United States*[26], has never been overruled on legal grounds and is still good case law.

The Constitution contemplated traditional wars lasting several years at the most. Our constitutional checks and balances were not set up to handle the stress of decades of War Time Constitution. Combine this with rapidly changing technology that allows government to destroy our privacy and other rights, and there simply are not sufficient limits upon government for the safety and security of our rights and liberties. Leave any man or group of men with undue power for too long, and they will abuse it. Basically, we need some sort of check and balance against permanent War Time Constitution, because at the moment, it does not appear that the current foreign threat will end.

18. **Redundancy**: In the event of a successful military or terrorist attack on Washington, D.C., we would have a ready body of elected leaders to replace representatives killed in any such attack. With the third division of Congress actually meeting in 435 different places across the country, it is unlikely an attack will effect more than a few districts. We could quickly rebuild our government in event of such a tragedy, and foil any attempt to weaken our nation by eliminating the sitting government.

19. **Update Out-of-Date Clauses Regarding Minimum National Security Requirements for Congress**: Article I, section 2, paragraph 2 of the U.S. Constitution sets forth that House members must be a Citizen of the United States for seven years, but contains **no requirement that someone running for the House of Representatives ever actually reside in the United States**. Article I, section 3, paragraph 3 provides that **Senators** must be a Citizen of the United States for nine years, but again there is **no residency requirement**. Compare this with the requirements to run for President at Article II, section 1, paragraph 5, which require the President to have been a Citizen since birth and requires the President to have been a Resident within the United States for 14 years.

The lack of residency requirements for House members and Senators is probably now a defect. In this age of guerilla terrorism, the current U.S. Constitution would allow a person to run for office if they were born here but lived most of their life in a foreign county. The original qualification standards were written in 1787, and should be updated to reflect the nature of changes over time in population, technology and warfare.

Suggested additional amendment #1: No person shall be a Representative of the House of Representatives who shall not have been a Citizen and Resident of the United States for at least 14 years (would revise Art. I, § 2, ¶2.)

Suggested additional amendment #2: No person shall be a Member of the Senate who shall not have been a Citizen and Resident of the United States for at least 18 years. (would revise Art. I, §3, ¶3.)

Suggested additional amendment #3: No person shall be eligible to the Office of President or Vice-President who shall not have been a natural born Citizen and Resident within the United States for at least 20 years (would revise Art. II, §1, ¶5.)

[Shorthand: For national security purposes, these clauses would add a requirement of aggregate residency within the United States for House members and Senators, and increase such requirement for the President and Vice-President.]

With the exception of the above discussion regarding the Second Amendment Right to Keep and Bear Arms, I have purposely avoided some of the more controversial topics that people raise as possible constitutional amendments. In my mind, all of those topics would be fair game at any Article V convention, and it could be healthy for the nation to see that discussion take place among careful, courteous leaders. However, I caution everyone that if it does not look like there is any possibility to get three-quarters of the states (38 of 50) to ratify such an amendment, it should not be used to block essential reforms.

CHAPTER 7

"Of, By, and For the People"

*"The basis of our political systems is the right of the people
to make and to alter their constitutions of government . . . .
The very idea of the power and the right of the people
to establish government presupposes the duty of every
individual to obey the established government"*[1]

(GEORGE WASHINGTON'S FAREWELL ADDRESS, SEPTEMBER 19, 1796)

THE CORE MEANING OF THE phrase "of, by and for the People" is that we have the right to make **and alter** our Constitution and form of government. If the power and right of the American People to make changes to their Constitution and government is not secure, the duty of the American People to obey the established government is likewise not secure.

As we have discussed, the Article V convention right of the people does not exist. It is an illusion. Article V gives the appearance of a convention right, but the Constitution is completely devoid of even a skeletal structure for choosing delegates and getting a convention started. We now must get smart enough to vote in state legislators who promise to call for an Article V convention and force ourselves to work these issues out. We need agreement on a system for choosing delegates consistent with democratic and republican principles.

OF THE PEOPLE

As far as making the Constitution goes, only 55 people participated in the Constitutional Convention of 1787.[2] The proceedings were secret.[3] To get a seat at the Convention, one needed to share four characteristics. You needed to be wealthy, white, Christian and male. No women had a seat at the table. No Hispanics, no Blacks, and no Asians were invited. No disabled were there, and no gays (that we know.) Even an amateur can read the Constitution and see the bias in favor of the Framers' socio-economic status.

BY THE PEOPLE

Not only did working class white Christian males not have a seat at the table at our nation's Constitutional Convention of 1787, most could not vote either. Working class white men could not vote in a majority of the states. Many of the early states required a man to own property as a qualification of suffrage.

1790 PROPERTY REQUIREMENTS TO HOLD OFFICE AND PROPERTY AND POLL TAX REQUIREMENTS TO VOTE

Many Americans assume that except for Americans derived from the African continent, working class Americans were treated equally during the years that our Constitution and Bill of Rights were written and approved (1787-1791, see Table 1: *State Ratifications of United States Constitution*, at page 8, and Table 2: *State Ratifications of Bill of Rights*, at page 8.) In reality, American workers were excluded from voting and holding office by state laws which imposed property ownership as a condition for both voting and holding office. Working class Americans did not have "a seat at the table" during the Constitutional Convention of 1787 or during the First Congress of the United States when the Bill of Rights was written.

Article I, Section 2, paragraph 1 of the United States Constitution provides:

> The House of Representatives shall be composed of Members <u>chosen</u> every second Year <u>by the People of the several States, and the Electors</u> <u>[voters] in each State shall have the Qualifications requisite for Electors</u> <u>[voters] of the most numerous Branch of the State Legislature.</u>[4]

This clause near the very beginning of the U.S. Constitution required that to vote in the national election, one must qualify to vote in the election for the largest chamber of such person's state legislature under state law.

Most of the states at that time also had property requirements to hold office. Working class Americans were prohibited from holding office by economic rules.

In 1790, some of the first fourteen states had no property ownership requirements to run for office or to vote, including Pennsylvania, Vermont, Connecticut and Rhode Island.[5] Virginia had no property requirement to vote, but did have a property ownership requirement to hold office.[6]

The property requirements to vote during that period were some-times different depending on whether a person was voting for the lower state house or upper state house. States which had the same property ownership condition to vote for either state house included New Jersey, Massachusetts, New Hampshire, Vermont, Georgia and South Carolina.[7] Their voting requirements were as follows[8]:

New Jersey	Owned real property worth at least £50 (roughly $18,750[9])
Massachusetts	Owned real property worth at least £60 (roughly $22,500)
New Hampshire	Poll tax
Vermont	Freemen only
Georgia	Paid taxes
South Carolina	Owned 50 acres or paid 3 shilling tax

The following states had different voting requirements for the upper and lower houses of their state legislature:

New York: Lower House: Owned real property worth £20
                    ($7,500), or providing rent of 40 shilling
                    Upper House: Owned real property worth £100
                    ($37,500)
North Carolina: Lower House: Freemen paying taxes only
                    Upper House: Owned at least 50 acres
Delaware: Lower House: Owned a freehold estate (a fee simple
                    or life estate in real property)
                    Upper House: Not specified in state constitution
Maryland: Lower House: Owned at least 50 acres
                    Upper House: Chosen by electoral college

Historian David S. Lutz, in his 1980 book, *Popular Consent and Popular Control*, states: "During the last half of the seventeenth century, suffrage restrictions increasingly tended to confine the vote to Protestant males who had property and were free, white, twenty-one, and native born."[6] Estimates are that from 25% to 50% of adult white males were not eligible to vote.[7] Not only were women denied the right to vote, but so was much of the working class, irrespective of skin tone.

The property requirements to hold office were much higher. Working class individuals were essentially prohibited through property qualification rules from holding office. Ten states imposed property ownership as a condition to run for office, as follows:[8]

Virginia   Lower House – own a freehold estate
                    Upper House – own a freehold estate
New Jersey &   Lower House – own real property worth at least £500
                    ($187,500)
Maryland   Upper House – own real property worth at least £1000
                    ($375,000)
Delaware   Upper House – own a freehold estate
North Carolina   Lower House – own at least 100 acres
                    Upper House – own at least 300 acres in fee

New York	Upper House – own real property worth at least £100 ($37,500)
Massachusetts	Lower House – own real property worth at least £100 ($37,500)
	Upper House – own real property worth at least £300 ($112,500), or have an estate taxed at least £60 ($22,500)
New Hampshire	Lower House – own real property worth at least £100 ($37,500)
	Upper House – own real property worth at least £200 ($75,000)
Georgia	Lower House – own at least 200 acres or real property worth at least £150 ($56,250)
	Upper House – own at least 250 acres or real property worth at least £250 ($93,750)
South Carolina	Lower House – own at least 500 acres plus ten "negroes", or real property worth at least £150 ($56,250)
	Upper House – own real property worth at least £300 ($112,500), clear of debt

FOR THE PEOPLE

Per former Senator Everett Dirksen:

> The very term "free state" means a free exchange of information, ideas, and facts from which responsible judgments can be made. **There must also be present the constitutional right of the people** to censure their government at the polls or, if need be, **to change the Constitution so as to alter the form of government – which right has always in our republic been vested in the people**. This right of the people to decide is founded on the premise that the decision is based on free discussion among free individuals. Only in this fashion, **only so long as this right is retained, can the people remain sovereign**.[9]

Congress has known for over fifty years that there are major drafting problems with the Article V Convention Clause. In reality, the American People do not have the right to alter their form of government due primarily to the flaw of having no procedure or remedy to choose delegates to a future convention.

The illusory Article V convention right is similar, for example, to a situation where a couple is getting divorced. Assume the husband had paid for his wife to become a Doctor, and now she has "run off" with a younger guy. In divorce proceedings, the wife has a lawyer but the husband does not. In settlement discussions, since he paid for the medical license for his wife, the husband demands that he get one-half of his soon to be ex-wife's medical license. His wife's attorney, knowing that it is against public policy to allow a medical license to be transferred, writes up the divorce documents saying that the husband will get one-half of the wife's medical license. The husband's "right" to practice medicine with half of a medical license would be illusory, as a transfer against public policy.

Another example might be an employee settling a case with an employer. The employee asks for a clause to be put in the agreement that says the employee will owe no taxes as a result of the money he or she will receive pursuant to the agreement. The employer includes such a clause but adds another that says that in the event the employee should be taxed, the employer will not be responsible for any of the employee's taxes. The employee's "right" to not pay taxes would be illusory. Public policy does not allow private parties to agree that taxes are not owed.

While small percentages of the legal profession, scholars and politicians are on notice of the Article V Convention Clause defect, the vast majority of the million or so American lawyers are not yet aware of the problem. We have never had an Article V convention so the issue has never come up in case law. Now is the time to make sure not just the legal profession is aware of the problem, but the entire nation as well. By proposing a skeletal structure along the lines of The Tricameralism Amendment, I am hoping to steer the country in the direction needed. The proposed amendment seeks to rectify the most basic issues – adequate representation and a clear process for amendment.

CHAPTER 8

Don't Fear the "Runaway" Convention

*"[A] bad feature in government, becomes
more and more fixed every day."*[1]

(Edmund Randolph, to Virginia House
of Delegates, October 10, 1787)

The American People have at times been scared away from having a
Constitutional Convention by the warning that it may turn into a "runaway
convention." Both the movement toward a balanced budget amendment
and the movement to reverse the "one person, one vote" decisions of the
U.S. Supreme Court fizzled when state legislators realized the Constitution
probably does not allow single topic conventions. The immediate answer
is that the Convention cannot run away because the convention delegates
only have the power to <u>propose</u> amendments to the Constitution. A for-
midable check and balance is written into Article V itself. **Three-fourths
of the states must vote to ratify any proposed amendment before it
becomes part of the Constitution.** Per Article V, proposed amendments,
whether proposed by Congress or by an Article V convention, "shall be
valid to all Intents and Purposes, as Part of this Constitution, when ratified
by the Legislatures of three fourths of the several States, or by Conventions
in three fourths thereof, as the one or the other Mode of Ratification may
be proposed by the Congress . . ."[2]

When voting to start a Constitutional Convention, each state gets only one vote. Likewise, when voting to approve a proposed constitutional amendment, each state gets just one vote. (See Article V of U.S. Constitution.) This fact alone is a reflection that the Framers of the Constitution did not think through the Convention Clause before they approved it. A one state, one vote rule results in wildly unequal and undemocratic results. (See Table 5: *Weakness of a California Citizen's Vote for a Constitutional Convention and to Approve Constitutional Amendments*, at pages 100-101.)

The population inequality in the U.S. Senate is offset with population equality in the U.S. House of Representatives. In our legislative system, there is only one stage of inequality – the Senate with its equal voting power for each state. The Article V convention process contains two unequal stages of equal state voting power, the "bookends" of starting an Article V convention and of ratifying proposed amendments. The Framers could not possibly have intended to make a democratic government only to return the process to undemocratic principles in convention. The only acceptable rule of voting for delegates to an Article V convention will be a one person, one vote rule. As it turns out, "one person, one vote" is the law of the land under the Equal Protection Clause when the Constitution does not provide a different rule.[3]

The inequality under a "one state, one vote" rule is obvious. Former Vice-President Richard Cheney lives in Wyoming. As reflected in Table 5 (using 2010 Census figures,) Dick Cheney and his fellow 568,158 Wyoming citizens get one vote for commencing an Article V constitutional convention **and** ratifying proposed constitutional amendments, while the 37,691,012 citizens of California also get just one vote to both call for a constitutional convention and to ratify proposed amendments. In other words, **each Californian's vote** for a Constitutional Convention is **worth only 1.5% of Dick Cheney's vote.** It is obviously **extremely anti-democratic.** The effect is that Wyoming citizen **Dick Cheney's voting power is 66⅓ times stronger than the voting power of a California citizen** in relation to calling a constitutional convention and ratifying amendments.

Table 5: *Weakness of a California Citizen's Vote for a Constitutional Convention and to Approve Constitutional Amendments (2010 census)*

State	Population And Number of Citizens Required to Obtain Only One Vote For Convention Purposes	State's Vote for Both a Constitutional Convention AND To Ratify Proposed Constitutional Amendments	Ratio (Weakness) of California Citizen's Vote Compared to Other States' Citizens To Call For Constitutional Convention AND to Ratify Proposed Constitutional Amendments
California	37,691,012	1	1
Texas	25,674,681	1	1.47
New York	19,465,197	1	1.93
Florida	19,057,542	1	1.98
Illinois	12,869,257	1	2.92
Pennsylvania	12,742,886	1	2.96
Ohio	11,544,951	1	3.26
Michigan	9,876,187	1	3.82
Georgia	9,815,210	1	3.84
North Carolina	9,656,401	1	3.9
New Jersey	8,821,155	1	4.27
Virginia	8,096,604	1	4.66
Washington	6,830,038	1	5.52
Massachusetts	6,587,536	1	5.72
Indiana	6,516,922	1	5.78
Arizona	6,482,505	1	5.81
Tennessee	6,403,353	1	5.89
Missouri	6,010,688	1	6.27
Maryland	5,828,289	1	6.47
Wisconsin	5,711,767	1	6.6
Minnesota	5,344,861	1	7.05
Colorado	5,116,769	1	7.37
Alabama	4,802,740	1	7.85

State	Population		
South Carolina	4,679,230	1	8.06
Louisiana	4,574,836	1	8.24
Kentucky	4,369,356	1	8.63
Oregon	3,871,859	1	9.74
Oklahoma	3,791,508	1	9.94
Connecticut	3,580,709	1	10.53
Iowa	3,062,309	1	12.31
Mississippi	2,978,512	1	12.66
Arkansas	2,937,979	1	12.83
Kansas	2,871,238	1	13.13
Utah	2,817,222	1	13.38
Nevada	2,723,322	1	13.84
New Mexico	2,082,224	1	18.10
West Virginia	1,855,364	1	20.32
Nebraska	1,842,641	1	20.46
Idaho	1,584,985	1	23.78
Hawaii	1,374,810	1	27.42
Maine	1,328,188	1	28.38
New Hampshire	1,318,194	1	28.59
Rhode Island	1,051,302	1	35.85
Montana	998,199	1	37.76
Delaware	907,135	1	41.55
South Dakota	824,082	1	45.74
Alaska	722,718	1	52.15
North Dakota	683,932	1	55.11
Vermont	626,431	1	60.17
Wyoming	568,158	1	66.34
TOTALS	308,745,538	50	

Calculating the numbers to compare Alaska, former Vice-Presidential candidate Sarah Palin's home state (population 722,718) with California, **a California citizen's vote for a Constitutional Convention is worth only 1.9% of Sarah Palin's vote** for the same. **Sarah Palin** (and her fellow state citizens,) in effect, **gets 52 votes for a Constitutional Convention compared to each California citizen's vote.**

Only 17 states are needed to block a convention call, while only 13 states are needed to prevent a proposed amendment from becoming part of the U.S. Constitution. Again, the calculations reflect an **unbalanced and anti-democratic system**.

The populations of the 13 smallest states adds up to 13,830,776 people in a nation (in 2010) of 308,745,538. Many people are misled by the language of the Constitution to believe that it would take one-fourth of the nation to block a proposed Constitutional amendment and one-third of the nation to prevent the start of an Article V convention. In reality, calculating the numbers **using democratic one person/one vote principles, just under 4.5% of the population can block a proposed Constitutional amendment from being ratified. It would take less than ten percent, only 7.6%, of the nation's population, to block a Constitutional Convention**, even if the entirety of 92% of the rest of the nation demanded it.

On top of the difficult burden established by Article V, we also have the issue of constitutional malpractice due to the fact that Article V does not specify how delegates to a future Article V convention will be chosen. Assuming we are able to work these issues out, the delegates themselves will have to agree to rules and procedures for the convention, another burden of inertia that could prevent a necessary amendment.

The 75% threshold for ratifying amendments, along with the other checks and balances involved, has caused the U.S. Constitution to be described as "the most difficult to amend of any constitution currently existing in the world today."[4]

Some will argue that Article V was intended to make it difficult to amend the U.S. Constitution. However, again and again, we have seen that the intent of the Framers was to find a "Goldilocks' Zone" of amendment, not too hard and not too easy. In the Federalist Number 43, James Madison wrote: "It guards equally against that extreme facility, which would render the Constitution too mutable, and that extreme difficulty, which might perpetuate its discovered faults."[5] Our Constitution was the first in the world to attempt to strike the right ratification balance for amending a constitution – the choices were not made through experience but gut instinct.[6] As it turns out, the bar chosen for amendment is too high. As a result, its errors learned through time and experience are "perpetuated."[7] We do not need fear the runaway convention. We need to fear never having a convention.

What even scholars typically forget to point out is that there is another strong check and balance within Article V, the amendment article of the U.S. Constitution. Article V gives Congress the power to propose constitutional amendments as well. Congress is a permanently sitting body and can easily transform itself into a sitting convention any time it chooses. Congress can offer competing amendments as a check and balance to the convention's proposals. The competing proposals might be weaker or stronger than those proposed through convention, or could be supplements to address problems overlooked by the convention. If people become concerned that the Constitutional Enclaves, acting as the format for an Article V convention, have too much power, Congress can offer amendments to the state legislatures to limit and "check and balance" them. Congress, if supported by 38 state legislatures, could even propose shutting down an Article V convention through the constitutional amendment process.[8]

Congress also has a similar type of "bully pulpit" as the President. Recently, Senators have even participated in "old school" filibusters, talking throughout the night to impress upon the American People their point of view. The House of Representatives and Senate could display their wisdom, experience and virtue to the American People, and convince us not to follow a poor choice (assuming the American People do not see the current Congress as so corrupt that the American People are no longer willing to listen to them.)

There is another check and balance within Article V, which is the power of the U.S. Congress to choose whether a proposed amendment will be sent for ratification to the state legislatures or to state ratification conventions. This was meant to allow Congress to avoid the state legislatures controlling too much of the amendment process by diverting the ratification power to the People of each state sitting in convention.

If state legislators want a check and balance over an Article V convention, the best manner to achieve such is for the state legislatures to agree to pay the costs of the convention. If the federal government does not agree to provide the buildings and security needed, the states can provide infrastructure for the convention. "Who pays," in constitution making, is a structural element.[9] State legislatures could threaten to withdraw necessary funds and have the check and balance of "closing the purse." The problem with this approach is that it is seen as a way to control the Article V Convention of the People, and would not be tolerated by large swaths of the citizenry. Nonetheless, the People will probably tolerate the state legislatures paying for the costs of the convention if the state legislatures should volunteer.

The concept of a runaway convention is a myth. What we really need to fear is a runaway President, Congress, Supreme Court, militarized and secretive law enforcement, and a corporate dominated economy. We should fear our state legislators being ignorant of their role in our federal system to call an Article V convention to correct for defects taught by experience and to check and balance corrupt or out of control national government.

We should fear leaders not thinking in advance what is needed for a proper Article V convention to propose constitutional amendments. The People's interest is in a successful convention. We will want to provide the convention delegates with all of the support they need to do an excellent job for us.

The original 1787 Convention needed to conceive, prepare and write an entirely new government formulation. Privacy was at a premium. The downside to such an approach is that the American public, including the many great minds within it, have no chance to review, comment and improve upon the work of the convention. The Article V convention is to propose amendments. We may very well come up with the best amendments through a more wide-open approach, where the public is given time to comment upon contemplated proposals for amendment. Through a public comment procedure, we can improve and refine our amendments to maximize the possibility for ratification. A broader, more inclusive approach, such as that suggested in Chapter 5, seems to make sense.

CHAPTER 9

The Article V Convention Makes Its Own Rules

*"Mr. Madison remarked on the vagueness of the terms,
'call a Convention for the purpose' as sufficient reason
for reconsidering the article. How was a Convention to be
formed? by what rule decide? what the force of its acts?"*[1]

(JAMES MADISON'S NOTES, PARAPHRASING HIMSELF, U.S.
CONSTITUTIONAL CONVENTION, SEPTEMBER 10, 1787.)

*"He saw no objection however against providing for a Convention
for the purpose of amendments, except only that difficulties might
arise as to the form, the quorum &c. which in Constitutional
regulations ought to be as much as possible avoided."*[2]

(JAMES MADISON'S NOTES, PARAPHRASING HIMSELF, U.S.
CONSTITUTIONAL CONVENTION, SEPTEMBER 15, 1787.)

AS OUR NATION BEGINS TO move toward an Article V convention, we must
be vigilant of our right and power over the Article V convention process.
In constitutional interpretation, the Article V convention is unique. By
understanding the special nature of Article V, we will be able to better
protect our rights.

The Preamble, "We the People," has real meaning and effect on the Article V Convention Clause analysis[3]. Instead of looking at the checks and balances between the branches, we are looking at an untested check and balance between the People and our entire United States government. The Supreme Court has never had a chance to opine regarding the Article V Convention Clause, except peripherally when discussing congressionally proposed amendments. Again, without a general agreement regarding how delegates to a convention are chosen, the Article V convention is an illusory right, a right which does not exist because we cannot start a constitutional convention without an agreed representation system.

There has been recent activity toward a constitutional convention under Article V. It calls itself the "Convention of the States" movement. It is a misnomer. Pursuant to the terms of the U.S. Constitution, an Article V convention will be a Convention of the People.

The reason to distrust the "Convention of the States" movement is that it literally is not on the side of the People. The "Convention of the States" leadership has duped state legislators into thinking that state legislatures choose delegates to any future Article V convention, rather than the People electing their own representatives to a convention. Legislative appointment of Article V convention delegates would be contrary to the text, structure, history, intent and purpose of Article V, as read together with the rest of the U.S. Constitution. As part of our basic system of separation or powers, States simply have no power over the federal system unless the Constitution grants such power. There is an Elections Clause which give states some power over legislative elections, but no such clause in Article V. The reason is obvious – as stated by Alexander Hamilton in the Federalist No. 59: "Nothing can be more evident, than that an exclusive power of regulating elections for the National Government, in the hands of the State Legislatures, would leave the existence of the Union entirely at their mercy." [4]

My advice to my fellow Americans is to join in and make the call for an Article V convention, but when you make your voice heard, teach your fellow Americans at the same time. Promote and advocate for an Article V convention, subject to these democratic and republican principles:

1. Delegates to any Article V convention must be **elected by the People**, not appointed by state legislatures.
2. Delegate selection will be based on a **"one person, one vote" system**, not "one state, one vote" and not an electoral college format.
3. **No limits** will be placed upon an Article V convention as to topic or time, other than the limits which the delegates themselves place on the convention.

I add a fourth principle for an Article V convention, to address the issue of vote and representation dilution caused by our nation's (and planet's) rapid population growth and the original failure to complete the Bill of Rights with a Size of Congress Amendment:

4. Representation of the American People at an Article V convention must be **meaningful representation**, in the range of one delegate/representative per 30,000 to 60,000 inhabitants.

These principles are what make an Article V convention a "Convention of the People," as intended by the Founding Generation, rather than a "Convention of the States."

If all Americans understood that the basic concept of **popular sovereignty** guides interpretation of the Article V Convention Clause, Americans can arm themselves with knowledge and acquire the ability to do an Article V convention analysis on their own. Popular sovereignty is the concept "that **sovereign power remains with the people, not with their government**."[5]

Once one understands the basic concept of popular sovereignty, and its effect on how the Article V Convention Clause is interpreted, most of you will be able to look at individual issues relating to a convention to propose amendments to the Constitution and draw the same conclusions, because you will be using the same standard – that standard which most closely fits the concept of popular sovereignty.

The primary concept to be learned is that an Article V convention is not a "Convention of the States," but obviously a "Convention of the People." The primary effect is that neither the U.S. Congress nor the state legislatures can limit an Article V convention.

CAN AN ARTICLE V CONVENTION BE LIMITED BY THE U.S. CONGRESS OR THE STATE LEGISLATURES?

The simple answer is no. However, this is one of the main disputes, learned through experience, that has arisen since the beginning of a movement for an Article V convention in the 1960's, after the Supreme Court decisions requiring a one person, one vote system in both chambers of state legislatures.[6]

Can an Article V convention be limited to only one topic, such as an amendment to balance the national budget? The text of Article V is not completely clear. It is a convention to propose amendments to the Constitution, using the plural "amendments." At the Federal Convention of 1787, the early clause was singular, but changed to plural.[7] The change reflects the thought and intent of the Framers that an Article V convention has the power to discuss and propose amendments in general, and cannot be limited to just one amendment desired by the states. The Supreme Court in the 2001 case of *Cook v. Gralike*, 531 U.S. 510 (2001), made clear that state legislatures may not limit Congress' power to propose constitutional amendments. The same rule applies to delegates sitting in convention – they have full power to propose amendments without limit by state legislatures or Congress.

The state legislatures can still get the one amendment they want, they just cannot limit an Article V convention to proposing just that amendment. The states' check and balance is in the last stage of the process – the ratification stage. Thirty-eight states (three-fourths) need to ratify a proposed amendment before it can become part of the Constitution. The states can simply ratify the amendment or amendments they want and reject all other proposals.

This view is supported further by other changes made to Article V at the 1787 Convention before the clause was finalized. On both September 10 and September 15, 1787, James Madison expressed concerns about adding a convention clause without some skeletal procedural architecture, especially with regard to the representation system for a convention (see quotes under this chapter's heading.) On September 10, 1787, Madison proposed and the convention delegates approved language that would have eliminated the Convention Clause and allowed the state legislatures to propose amendments directly with the other states:

> "<u>The Legislature of the U. S.</u> whenever two thirds of both Houses shall deem necessary, or <u>on the application of two thirds of the Legislatures of the several States, shall propose amendments to this Constitution,</u> which shall be valid to all intents and purposes as part thereof, when the same shall have been ratified by three fourths at least of the Legislatures of the several States, or by Conventions in three fourths thereof, as one or the other mode of ratification may be proposed by the Legislature of the U. S."[8]

At the end of the last work day of the Convention, September 15, 1787, a constitutional convention clause was written back into the Constitution. Colonel Mason "thought the plan of amending the Constitution exceptionable & dangerous."[9] Delegates Morris and Gerry then "moved to amend the article so as to require a Convention on application of ⅔ of the [states.]"[10] Madison warned the delegates "that difficulties might arise as to the form, the quorum [etc.] which in Constitutional regulations ought to be as much as possible avoided."[11] The Convention delegates appear from the record to ignore Madison's warning and approved the Article V convention as the alternative path to proposing constitution amendments rather than the state legislatures having the power to offer amendments directly. The motion to reinsert the convention alternative for amendments, literally made as the end of the 1787 Convention, passed without opposition.[12]

The change was obviously meant to take some power over the alternative amendment process from the state legislatures and instead place the power to propose amendments closer to the People, sitting in convention. The change followed the discussion about the amending clause, where the delegates seemed to agree that neither the U.S. Congress nor the state legislatures should have the ability to control the entire amendment process. On September 10, 1787, delegate Elbridge Gerry of Massachusetts reacted to the "bare bones" convention clause which came out of the Committee of Detail: "On the application of the Legislatures of two thirds of the States in the Union, for an amendment of this Constitution, the Legislature of the United States shall call a Convention for that purpose." Gerry was concerned that two-thirds of the states could damage the other states by changing the U.S. Constitution.[13]

Alexander Hamilton shared concerns about the clause as written, but from the point of view that he did not want to see the state legislatures use the process to take away power from a strong central government. James Madison's amendment on September 10, 1787 attempted to address both views by requiring three-fourths of the states to ratify any proposed amendments and giving the U.S. Congress, with respect to an Article V convention, the alternative of sending proposals for amendment not to the state legislatures but to state ratifying conventions. This is an important piece of evidence as to what was envisioned for the convention alternative for amendment. Constitutional conventions, not legislatures, were seen at the time as being closest to the People.[14] The concept of a convention alternative not just to propose amendments, but a convention alternative within the states to ratify the amendments, was seen as a check and balance against state legislatures having too much control over the amendment process.

From the beginning of the 1787 Convention, the concept introduced by the Virginia Plan with respect to amending the Constitution remained as one of the goals of the amending clause: "That provision ought to be made for the amendment of the Articles of Union whensoever it shall seem necessary, and that **the assent of the National Legislature ought not to be required thereto.**"[15] Recall that early in the 1787 Convention, on June 11, 1787, Colonel George Mason of Virginia, one of only three delegates who refused to sign the new Constitution, spoke in support of such clause, expressing that "[i]t would be improper to require the consent of the [National] Legislature, because they may abuse their power, and refuse their consent on that very account."[16] Nothing in the record reflects a rejection of this position by the assembly. To the contrary, the record reflects the delegates working toward this as one of the goals of the amending clause. (See Appendix 3: *Article V Revision History During Constitutional Convention*.) Then, on the last work day of the Convention, September 15, 1787, Mason stated his concern even more forcefully when he expressed that if all amendments were to rely on Congress, "no amendments of the proper kind would ever be obtained by the people, if the Government should become oppressive, as he verily believed would be the case."[17]

The concept ultimately followed by the Convention delegates was that neither the U.S. Congress nor the state legislatures have a "free run" at changing the Constitution.

If the state legislatures were able to 1) vote for the start of the convention, 2) control who could be a delegate at the convention (including choosing themselves,) and 3) control the ratification process as well, the state legislatures would have the power to do what Article V was intended not to do – give the state legislatures control over all major phases of the amending process. The need to prevent states from attempting to control the federal system is so strong that Article I, Section 10 of the Constitution prohibits states from entering into agreements with each other without the consent of Congress. Accordingly, when we interpret Article V, we look to see if it is possible under certain interpretations for the state legislatures to "run the table" of the amending process. If so, something is wrong with the interpretation.

Likewise, an interpretation which allows any control or limit by the U.S. Congress over an Article V convention is also wrong. Our interpretation must take into account both purposes of the Framers.

We have been discussing the intent and purpose behind the convention alternative in Article V. Constitutional analysis, however, starts with an analysis of the text. Textual analysis (and structural analysis) in this instance is consistent with the intent and purpose behind the Article V Convention Clause. The power to propose amendments in a constitutional convention is textually assigned to the Article V convention, not to the state legislatures and not to Congress.

The text provides four basic stages, with the omitted stage of electing delegates assumed, for five basic stages:

1. Two-thirds of state legislatures vote for Article V convention.
2. **Convention delegates are elected (by The People, not appointed by state legislatures.)**
3. The Convention forms, prepares rules, makes proposals, debates and deliberates, votes and proposes constitutional amendments.
4. Proposals go to U.S. Congress before going to the states; Congress decides whether ratification will be by three-fourths of state legislatures or three-fourths of state ratification conventions.
5. When three-fourths of the states, through whichever mode of ratification is chosen, vote to ratify a proposed amendment, it becomes part of the U.S. Constitution.[18]

We apply the two amendments of the Bill of Rights which were added as standards for interpretation, the 9th and 10th Amendments. First, the Tenth Amendment:

Tenth Amendment, United States Constitution
The powers not delegated to the United States by the Constitution, nor prohibited by it to the States, are reserved to the States respectively, or to the people.

The Tenth Amendment is the Doctrine of Enumerated Powers[19], also called the Doctrine of Limited Government Power. States demanded such principle be stated as an amendment to the Constitution.[20] With respect to Article V, without knowing its history and purpose, the Tenth

Amendment lacks clarity as to which powers are reserved to the States and which powers are reserved to the people. What is clear, however, is that with the exception of the fourth stage of the process, the U.S. Constitution does not give the U.S. Congress any power over an Article V convention. On this point, there is broad scholarly agreement.[21]

The duty to "call" for the Article V convention after 34 states have communicated to Congress their vote for the call of the convention is just that – a ministerial duty requiring Congress to count and announce. The duty to count and announce gives Congress no power to limit the topics which can be discussed at an Article V convention nor does Congress have the power to limit how long an Article V convention can remain open. Yet, it is the language in Article V, that Congress "shall call a convention," that Republican senators relied upon in trying to take from the People our power over an Article V convention.[22] The constitutional convention procedures bills of the last century were an attempt by Congress to extend power over the People through overly extended interpretation of the Constitution.

The language of Article V itself is clear – Congress "shall call a convention . . ." The language is mandatory, not discretionary. When pressed on the issue, those supporting the "new" Constitution were clear that Congress has no such discretion. In The Federalist Number 85, Alexander Hamilton states:

> "**[T]he national rulers**, whenever nine States concur, **will have no option upon the subject. By the fifth article of the plan, the Congress will be obliged** 'on the application of the legislatures of two thirds of the States (which at present amount to nine), **to call a convention for proposing amendments,** which shall be valid, to all intents and purposes, as part of the Constitution, when ratified by the legislatures of three fourths of the States, or by conventions in three fourths thereof.' **The words of this article are peremptory. The Congress 'shall call a convention.' Nothing in this particular is left to the discretion of that body.**"[23]

The United States Supreme Court has made few comments in cases directly about the Article V Convention Clause. However, in the case of

United States v. Sprague[24], the Supreme Court acknowledged Congress' mandatory duty to call an Article V convention upon application of two-thirds of the state legislatures:

> "The United States asserts that Article V is clear in statement and in meaning, contains no ambiguity, and calls for no resort to rules of construction. A mere reading demonstrates that this is true. It provides two methods for proposing amendments. Congress may propose them by a vote of two-thirds of both houses, or, on the application of the legislatures of two-thirds of the states, **must call a convention** to propose them."[25]

At the 1787 Convention, Madison himself confirmed the understanding that the "convention call" is a mandatory duty of Congress: "Mr Madison did not see why Congress would not be as much bound to propose amendments applied for by two thirds of the States as to call a call a [sic] Convention on the like application."[26]

If Congress has a duty to call an Article V convention, must it call such a convention when two-thirds of state legislatures ask not for a general convention to propose amendments, but fashion their "applications" as a vote for a limited topic or "special interest" convention? On this issue, human bias guides even the minds of professors and lawyers. Viewpoints can differ wildly. Nonetheless, with study, the Constitution does provide an answer.

Recall from Chapter 3 the interchange between James Madison and Patrick Henry regarding the Preamble, when Henry challenged Madison regarding the meaning and effect of the words, "We the People." Madison's answer was as follows:

> "Should all the states adopt it, **it will be then a government established** by the thirteen states of America, not through the intervention of the legislatures, but **by the people at large**. In this particular respect, **the distinction between the existing and proposed governments is very material. The existing system**

has been derived from the dependent derivative authority of the legislatures of the states; whereas this is derived from the superior power of the people."[27]

The distinction is very material when looking at who has power over an Article V convention, the state legislatures or the People themselves. Recall that procedure, remedy and substantive rights are tied together. If either the U.S. Congress or the state legislatures had the power to impose procedures on the Article V convention, they could easily manipulate and abuse such power by setting up procedural rules which cut off or make much more difficult the ability to obtain amendments. In other words, by depriving the American People of their Article V remedy through procedural rules, government would deprive us of our Article V right and power as well.

Because the original meaning and intent of the Constitution, as reflected in the Preamble, was that the People have the superior power in our system, an Article V convention must be controlled by the People, not by the state legislatures. This is why an Article V convention is a Convention of the People, not a Convention of the States.

The powers delegated by the People to the national legislative branch are listed at Article I, Section 8 of the U.S. Constitution. Nowhere in such section is any power over an Article V convention given to the U.S. Congress. The last paragraph of Article I, Section 8 is the Necessary and Proper Clause, which gives Congress such implied powers as "shall be necessary and proper for carrying into Execution the foregoing Powers, **and all other Powers vested by this Constitution in the Government** of the United States, or in any Department or Officer thereof."[28] The question becomes whether Article V itself vests in Congress any powers over an Article V convention.

Initially, the text of the Necessary and Proper clause does not even appear to apply to the Article V Convention Clause. Power over the Article V convention itself is not vested in the U.S. Government or any of its departments or officers.

The Tenth Amendment was meant to address a specific problem. By listing a Bill of Rights, lawyers could argue the matter from two different views. One view would be that the People have <u>only</u> the rights listed in the

Constitution and the government has the power to legislate in any area not listed. The other view is that the government is limited in its powers, and the fact that a right is not listed in the Bill of Rights does not by itself convey power to government. The Tenth Amendment makes clear that if a power is not delegated to the United States by the Constitution, Congress cannot legislate or act in that area.

Despite the relatively settled issue that Congress has no power over an Article V convention[29], corrupt politicians will still make the argument that the duty "to call" the Article V convention is actually a power to control the convention as well. It would be a Congressional power grab by an improper expansion of the <u>interpretation</u> of the "shall call a convention" language of Article V. The Framers thought about this too, and cut off government power to expand its own power through expanded interpretation. The Founding Generation's answer to this was the Ninth Amendment.

As we bring the Ninth Amendment into the analysis, realize that because two-thirds of the state legislatures have never voted for the call of the Article V convention, many issues relating to an Article V convention will be **issues of first impression** that the United States Supreme Court will never have previously addressed. In Chapter 6, we discussed the second amendment case of *Washington D.C. v. Heller*[30]. The 2008 *Heller* case was a **case of first impression** by the Supreme Court as to whether there is an individual right to bear arms under the Second Amendment. The majority opinion and Justice Stevens' dissenting opinion in that case both went back and attempted to determine the original meaning and intent of the Second Amendment. While the viewpoints of how to interpret original meaning differed, all justices participated in interpreting original meaning. Because all issues relating to an Article V convention will also be issues of first impression, the Court will first attempt to determine the original meaning and intent of the Article V Convention Clause.

In order to do that, the Court will also have to go back and determine the original meaning of the Ninth Amendment.

Ninth Amendment, United States Constitution

The enumeration in the Constitution, of certain rights, shall not be construed to deny or disparage others retained by the people.

Per Professor Kurt Lash:

"The Tenth's [referring to the Tenth Amendment] declaration that all nondelegated and nonprohibited powers are reserved to the states assures that the federal government exercises only enumerated delegated powers. This declaration, however, does not prevent expansive *interpretations* of enumerated federal powers – interpretations which, if broad enough, would render meaningless the Tenth's reservation of powers to the states (state power having been supplanted by federal action). The danger of expansive interpretations of federal power did not escape the members of the state ratifying conventions who considered the original Constitution, and they insisted on adding a rule of construction that limited the interpretation of enumerated federal power. James Madison complied by drafting the Ninth Amendment. According to Madison, the purpose of the Ninth Amendment was to "[guard] against a latitude of interpretation" while the Tenth Amendment "exclud[ed] every source of power not within the constitution itself."[31]

One of the main barriers to ratifying the Constitution was the lack of a Bill of Rights. One of the primary concerns related to how to interpret the Constitution. Even if powers were limited, "sharp" lawyers and politicians could use the Necessary and Proper Clause[32] to expand power beyond the point that the People intended the government to have. Therefore, in addition to the Tenth Amendment "expressly declaring the principle of enumerated federal power, [the] principle [of the Ninth Amendment] would prevent any attempt to use the Necessary and Proper

Clause as justification for a federal government of general unenumerated power."[33]

When we go back and look at the original meaning of the Ninth and Tenth Amendments, we are presented with these concepts:

1. The Tenth Amendment limits the powers of the national government to only those powers stated in the Constitution; and
2. The Ninth Amendment prevents an expansive interpretation of national power which would constructively or impliedly enlarge government power beyond what is "necessary and proper."[34]

Per Professor Akhil Reed Amar:

> "[T]he most obvious and inalienable right underlying the Ninth Amendment is the collective right of We the People to alter or abolish government, through the distinctly American device of the constitutional convention."[35]

Because the Article V convention is the means to alter the form of our government when Congress is corrupt or will not act, the People, as sovereign, maintain the power and right over the Article V convention. Note that the Tenth Amendment speaks in terms of powers, while the Ninth speaks in terms of rights. Typically, we speak of government having power and the People having rights. The one situation where the People have retained an enumerated power is that of sitting in convention for the purpose of deciding whether to propose amendments to the U.S. Constitution. It is not only considered a power, but a right of the People as well. In George Washington's Farewell Address of September 19, 1796, he referred to the ability of the People to amend the Constitution as both a right and power:

> "The basis of our political systems is **the right** of the people **to make and to alter their constitutions of government** . . . . The very idea of **the power and the right of the people to establish**

government presupposes the duty of every individual to obey the established government."[36]

In Washington's Inaugural Address of April 30, 1789, he also referred to the Article V ability to amend the Constitution as a power:

"Besides the ordinary objects submitted to your care, it will remain with your judgment to decide, how far an exercise of the occasional **power delegated by the Fifth article of the Constitution** is rendered expedient at the present juncture by the nature of objections which have been urged against the System, or by the degree of inquietude which has given birth to them."[37]

The Ninth and Tenth Amendments were meant to help interpret the Article V Convention Clause. With respect to the Tenth Amendment and Article V, Congress' duty to call a convention after two-thirds of state legislatures vote for one is just that, a duty and not a power. There is no issue of unduly expanding government power over an Article V convention through the Necessary and Proper Clause because Congress has not been assigned any power over the Article V convention. As a result, Congress cannot limit the Article V convention in any manner. Moreover, the Ninth Amendment makes clear that to the extent the "call" of the convention is a power, the U.S. Congress shall not expansively interpret such power to deny or reduce the People's right to propose alterations to our Constitution in an Article V convention.

In addition, the structure of Article V itself reflects an intent by the Framers that the rights and powers of the American People over an Article V convention should be equal to the powers of Congress to propose amendments under Article V. Article V stands alone as its own article of the original Constitution. There is no three-branch check and balance structure for an Article V convention. Instead, we have a "bookend" check and balance structure, with state legislatures controlling the start of an Article V convention and state legislatures or state ratifying conventions controlling whether a proposed amendment becomes part of the Constitution. (See

Table 5: *Weakness of a California Citizen's Vote for a Constitutional Convention and to Approve Constitutional Amendments*, at pages 100-101.)
Per Professor Michael Stokes Paulsen:

> [T]he *structure* of the Article V text supports an inference that the convention must have plenary power to propose amendments on whatever subjects it deems appropriate. The convention-proposal method is worded in parallel with the congressional-proposal method, implying an equivalence of their proposing powers:
>
> "The Congress, whenever two thirds of both houses shall deem it necessary, shall propose Amendments to this Constitution, or, on the Application of the Legislatures of two thirds of the several States, shall call a Convention for proposing Amendments, which, in either Case, shall be valid to all Intents and Purposes, as Part of this Constitution, when ratified . . . ."
>
> There is no limitation on what amendments Congress may propose to the states. Since the convention method is a substitute for the congressional method, it presumably has an equivalent scope of authority and can no more be subject to limitation than Congress.[38]

Obviously, it would be an offense to the American People to think that Congress has unlimited power to propose constitutional amendments but that the People sitting in convention as sovereign do not. The structure of the Article V convention alternative itself reflects the Framers' intent. Congress is given the power to choose the mode of ratification, but is given no power to propose amendments in the Article V convention process.[39] This supports the purpose of the convention alternative of having a way to amend without the consent of Congress. "As such, Congress' power relating to Article V must be construed as narrowly as possible, so that the purpose of the convention of providing a means to circumvent Congress can be most fully realized."[40]

The final conclusion that neither the U.S. Congress nor the state legislatures can limit an Article V Convention of the People is based on a rather simple observation. The power of the U.S. Congress attaches to the Article

V process at the fourth stage, when proposals coming out of an Article V convention are sent to Congress for Congress to decide whether ratification will be by state legislatures or state ratification conventions. The process is not a mere "pass-through," where the Article V convention communicates proposed constitutional amendments to Congress and Congress simply passes the communication on to the states. Rather, the proposals "loop back" through Congress before proposals can be forwarded to the states. Congress now has to decide what route is better (or worse) for passage of the amendment proposal – state legislatures or state ratification conventions.

When Congressional power attaches to the process in the fourth stage[41], it disallows such Congressional power from limiting the People's Article V convention. The Ninth and Tenth Amendments guide the interpretation. **The Article V process involves a combination of state and national power. Because Congress cannot limit the convention, the state legislatures likewise cannot limit an Article V convention in conjunction with Congress**.

Referring back to the issue of the intent of the Framers that Article V is a general convention not limited by topic is again reflected in a letter from James Madison to Thomas Mann Randolph after the Constitution was ratified but before the First Congress could meet to prepare a Bill of Rights:

> "I have said, that I think the amendments ought to be undertaken by the Congress. I prefer that mode, to a **General Convention**, as most expeditious, most certain (since there are States who will object to the mode of a Convention, without being averse to amendments in themselves) as being most safe, and as most economical."[42]

From reading this passage, it is clear that the original view was that Article V provides for a general convention. If the states could limit an Article V convention to singular amendments, they would have no reason to object to the mode of Convention while not being against single amendment proposals from Congress.

Historically, the House of Representatives set the standard early that the Power to Propose Constitutional Amendments is not limited to proposing only amendments requested by the States. Just as the First Congress was beginning their work on July 21, 1789, and the House referred the work on the Bill of Rights to a select committee, the House also agreed that the "committee not be bound by state recommendations for Amendments."[43] Primary evidence of the use of this power is the Just Compensation Clause at the end of the Fifth Amendment, as no state legislature asked for such a clause. Furthermore, for the first one hundred years of our history, almost all state applications for an Article V convention called for a general convention.[44]

Finally, again looking at the purpose of the Article V convention, it is meant as a vehicle to reunite and bring the country back together. A general convention that allows all the freedom to at least make a public proposal promotes that purpose. If a convention were limited to a specific topic, it is, or at least gives the perception that it is, a special interest convention, would be perceived to favor only certain factions while leaving out others, and would likely be counterproductive to the interest of promoting unity. The fact that numerous groups did not have a seat at the original 1787 Convention is more reason to ensure that the First Article V Convention is a general convention, of the People.

ELECTIONS BY THE PEOPLE

In the final analysis, the failure of the Article V Convention Clause to provide a method for choosing delegates, combined with the effect of the Equal Protection Clause of the Fourteenth Amendment, leads to the inevitable conclusion that each and every American over the age of eighteen has the right to a seat and voice at the next Article V convention. There is no stadium or field to hold all of us. Republican principles guide us.[45] We must come up with a representation system and our individual right becomes a right to run for a seat as delegate. However, for the system to have acceptance by the People, there must be broadly based representation, as suggested in Chapter 5, which introduced The Tricameralism Amendment.

One of the biggest fights the People may have with our politicians is whether the People elect delegates to the Convention of the People, or state legislatures get to appoint the delegates. The rule guiding who gets to choose Article V delegates should be obvious. The standard most consistent with popular sovereignty is that of the People choosing their own representatives, especially for a constitutional convention.

It is essential in a free republic that the people choose their own representatives.[46] When returning to the fundamental law of a constitution of government, our tradition is to return the question to the People sitting in convention. After the Constitution was completed, the delegates resolved that the ratification of the Constitution should take place in state conventions with a special election by the People for the special purpose.[47] In the Federalist Number 39, Madison states: "[T]he Constitution is to be founded on the assent and ratification of the people of America, given by deputies elected for the special purpose . . ."[48] Madison cements the idea in the Federalist Number 49 that whenever we are dealing with the fundamental law, our Constitution, power flows from the People, and only the People in direct elections have the power to elect delegates to an Article V convention:

> "As the people are the only legitimate fountain of power, and it is from them that the constitutional charter, under which the several branches of government hold their power, is derived; it seems strictly consonant to the republican theory, to recur to the same original authority, not only whenever it may be necessary to enlarge, diminish or new-model the powers of government; but also, whenever any one of the departments may commit encroachments on the chartered authorities of the others."[49]

We also must meet the requirement that the state legislatures should not be able to control the entire amendment process. If state legislatures had the power to choose delegates to a constitutional convention, the state legislatures could control the entire process. They could literally choose themselves as the delegates, shutting the American People out of the process of amending our own government. Such would obviously be inconsistent with the intent, structure and purpose of Article V. The only acceptable standard is an election of delegates by the People.

Historically we have only ratified by state convention twice, for the original Constitution and for the Twenty-First Amendment.[50] Twenty-six of our twenty-seven constitutional amendments have been ratified by the state legislatures.[51] According to the Congressional Research Service, the option of a ratification convention to approve the original Constitution was considered to "be more democratic and more reflective of the public will than by state legislatures. State legislatures, it was assumed, would be less open to change, and more interested in preserving the status quo."[52] The trend of both the U.S. Congress and state legislatures has been to preserve the status quo. The guilty parties include the state legislators, for it is their duty to call for an Article V convention to correct basic errors in the check and balance system.

We are left with the state legislatures as the bookends of the convention path to amendment. The U.S. Constitution is a structural document, seeking to find the "Goldilocks' zone" of checks and balances. The fact that the state legislatures already 1) control whether a convention will even start, and 2) can control whether a proposed amendment will become law, dictates that the convention delegates be elected by the people rather than appointed by the state legislatures.

If the state legislatures are allowed to also pick the delegates to the convention, then the state legislatures can rule all three of the main power elements of the convention process: starting the convention, making the proposed amendments, and ratifying the amendments. They could pick themselves as delegates, propose amendments, and then ratify the amendments they just proposed. Part of our nation's "corruption problem" is that many of the state legislatures have been compromised by wealth and party politics in the same manner as the national legislature. It does not make sense from a check and balance standpoint that state legislatures would appoint Article V convention delegates, and it is not conceivable that such would have been intended by the Framers.

With respect to the Fourteenth Amendment, all three of its limits on the states must be taken into account:

"No State shall make or enforce any law which shall abridge the privileges or immunities of citizens of the United States; nor shall any State deprive any person of life, liberty, or property, without due process of law; nor deny to any person within its jurisdiction the equal protection of the laws."[53]

The Due Process Clause of the Fourteenth Amendment prohibits states from depriving persons of liberty or property without "due process of law." Changes made to the U.S. Constitution will affect the balancing of liberty interests, and may affect property interests as well. As a result, the procedure for an Article V Convention for proposing constitutional amendments must meet the requirements of due process.

The most basic elements of due process are notice and an opportunity to be heard.[54] As applied to the Article V Convention Clause analysis, elections by the People promote "the two central concerns of procedural due process, the prevention of unjustified or mistaken deprivations and the promotion of participation and dialogue by affected individuals in the decision-making process."[55]

"[R]epresentative government is in essence self-government through the medium of elected representatives of the people, and each and every citizen has an inalienable right to full and effective participation in the political processes of his State's [and nation's] legislative bodies. Most citizens can achieve this participation only as qualified voters through the election of legislators to represent them."[56]

In addition, as the right to elect our own representatives to an Article V convention is a fundamental right, it is also protected by the Privileges and Immunities Clause of the Fourteenth Amendment.

Elections by the People also provide the proper balance and national coverage expected of a convention for changing constitutional law. Such a gathering is expected to represent all voices. If state legislatures were allowed to appoint delegates, all would be political actors/full-time politicians. Also, you would get an imbalance toward the states, which is why changes were made at the original Constitutional Convention, on September 15, 1787. (See Appendix 3: *Article V Revision History During Constitutional Convention*.)

Elections by the People would result in at least some delegates who are respected members of the community but not known as full-time politicians. Scholars who would never run for office otherwise could run for this momentous occasion. We would also get some delegates more prone to maintaining strong national government, who would act as devil's advocates and a balance to make the final product better. The more neutral delegates would act as a mediating influence, which we would not likely get without elections by the People.

In the early 1970's, the American Bar Association made clear its disapproval of some of the gamesmanship seen in Congress at the time with respect to trying to legislate procedure for an Article V convention:

> We believe it of fundamental importance that a constitutional convention be representative of the people of the country. This is especially so when it is borne in mind that the method was intended to make available to the "people" a means of remedying abuses by the national government. If the convention is to be "responsive" to the people, then the structure most appropriate to the convention is one representative of the people. This, we believe, can only mean an election of convention delegates by the people. An election would help assure public confidence in the convention process by generating a discussion of the constitutional change sought and affording the people the opportunity to express themselves to the future delegates.[57]

Not only must an Article V convention be populated by representatives elected by the People, but as the American Bar Association has said, the representation must be "responsive" to the People. To do this, we must go back to the original proposed Bill of Rights and make sure that our Article V convention will have adequate and meaningful representation, in the general direction suggested by The Tricameralism Amendment as set forth in Chapter 5.

ONE PERSON, ONE VOTE ELECTION STANDARD

The standard most consistent with popular sovereignty is the standard that we have an equal vote – known as the "one person, one vote" standard. This is the law of the land when the constitution does not provide a different standard.[58]

When senators initially began trying to control the People's Article V convention rights, an attempt was made to use the standard utilized at the 1787 Convention – one state, one vote.[59] Any so-called "scholar" taking the position that an Article V convention would be a "one state, one vote" convention is not a real scholar. The Articles of Confederation had a one state, one vote rule.[60] The U.S. Constitution, through the Preamble, Article V and the Ninth, Tenth and Fourteenth Amendments, changed the rules.

Obviously, a one state, one vote system is highly undemocratic and inconsistent with the concept of sovereignty by the People. Table 5: *Weakness of a California Citizen's Vote for a Constitutional Convention and to Approve Constitutional Amendments* at pages 100-101 reflects how citizens in small states get more voting power at the beginning and end stages of the Article V convention process. For example, the citizens of Montana have more than 66 times the voting power of Californians in starting an Article V convention and in ratifying proposed constitutional amendments. Citizens of Alaska have 52 times the voting power of Californians for such purposes. Politicians were convinced to change their bill[61], but the change went to a type of electoral college format, adding two additional delegates to each state for each state's two senators.

Per the 1972 Harvard Law Review:

> "The result of this scheme is that the people of less populated states will have proportionately greater representation at the convention than the people of more populated states, despite the fact that the voters of the less populated states already carry more weight at the application and ratification stages."[62]

Table 6: *How the Electoral College "Waters Down" Votes of People Who Live in More Populous States* (at pages 130-131) reflects how an electoral college format, meant for the election of a single executive leader, would effect a broad-based representation system. Small states are favored.

When electing a single President, adding two votes for the two senators in each state gives more voting power to the small states and acts as a check and balance for the large states getting to vote all of their Electoral College votes in a block. There is no such equivalent in the Article V convention system. To the contrary, an electoral college format applied to an Article V convention serves to upset checks and balances by giving small states even more power with no offset in the check and balance structure.[63]

The fact is, the current state of constitutional law in the United States requires a one person, one vote standard.[64] The burden will be on politicians to convince people that an undemocratic rule should apply. As the current default rule is in the favor of the People's sovereignty, I do not see politicians ever meeting such burden.

Table 6: *How the Electoral College "Waters Down" Votes of People Who Live in More Populous States* (2010 census)

State	Population	Electoral Votes	State Citizens Required to get One Electoral Vote
California	37,691,012	55	685,307
Texas	25,674,681	38	675,650
New York	19,465,197	29	671,214
Florida	19,057,542	29	657,156
Illinois	12,869,257	20	643,463
Pennsylvania	12,742,886	20	637,144
Ohio	11,544,951	18	641,386
Michigan	9,876,187	16	617,262
Georgia	9,815,210	16	613,451
North Carolina	9,656,401	15	643,760
New Jersey	8,821,155	14	630,083
Virginia	8,096,604	13	622,816
Washington	6,830,038	12	569,170
Massachusetts	6,587,536	11	598,867
Indiana	6,516,922	11	592,447
Arizona	6,482,505	11	589,319
Tennessee	6,403,353	11	582,123
Missouri	6,010,688	10	601,069
Maryland	5,828,289	10	582,829
Wisconsin	5,711,767	10	571,177
Minnesota	5,344,861	10	534,486
Colorado	5,116,769	9	568,530
Alabama	4,802,740	9	533,638
South Carolina	4,679,230	9	519,914
Louisiana	4,574,836	8	571,855
Kentucky	4,369,356	8	546,170
Oregon	3,871,859	7	553,123
Oklahoma	3,791,508	7	541,644
Connecticut	3,580,709	7	511,530
Iowa	3,062,309	6	510,385
Mississippi	2,978,512	6	496,419
Arkansas	2,937,979	6	489,663
Kansas	2,871,238	6	478,540
Utah	2,817,222	6	469,537

Table 6: *How the Electoral College "Waters Down" Votes of People Who Live in More Populous States* (2010 census) (page 2)

State	Population	Electoral Votes	State Citizens Required to get One Electoral Vote
Nevada	2,723,322	6	453,887
New Mexico	2,082,224	5	416,445
West Virginia	1,855,364	5	371,073
Nebraska	1,842,641	5	368,548
Idaho	1,584,985	4	396,246
Hawaii	1,374,810	4	343,703
Maine	1,328,188	4	332,047
New Hampshire	1,318,194	4	329,549
Rhode Island	1,051,302	4	262,826
Montana	998,199	3	332,733
Delaware	907,135	3	302,378
South Dakota	824,082	3	274,694
Alaska	722,718	3	240,906
North Dakota	683,932	3	227,977
Vermont	626,431	3	208,810
Wyoming	568,158	3	189,386

As reflected in the graphic above, every 189,386 Wyoming citizens get one electoral vote for president and vice president of the United States, while every 685,307 California citizens get one electoral vote for president and vice president of the United States. In other words, each Californian's vote for president is worth only 27.6% of a Wyoming citizens vote. It is obviously extremely undemocratic.

Compared to each California citizen, the citizens of the following states have this many more votes for President and Vice President:

Wyoming	3.62 votes
Vermont	3.28 votes
North Dakota	3.01 votes
Alaska	2.84 votes
South Dakota	2.49 votes
Delaware	2.27 votes
Etc.	

Limits as to Topic or Subject Matter

The Article V convention cannot be limited as to what it can discuss or what amendments it can propose. The **power to propose amendments** was expressly placed in the hands of an Article V convention rather than the state legislatures.[65] Per Professor Walter Dellinger, "[i]f the aim had been to give the state legislatures the power to propose as well as to ratify amendments, it would have been unnecessary to provide for conventions."[66] Furthermore, there can be no argument of state police power coming into play, as the Article V convention is a unique procedure in history, meant to replace the prior sovereign with the People, and no state by itself ever had power over a national convention[67].

As referenced earlier in this chapter, Congress established on July 21, 1789 that the power to propose constitutional amendments is not "bound by state recommendations for Amendments."[68] The Supreme Court confirmed this rule in the 2001 case of Cook v. Gralike, 531 U.S. 510 (2001).

An Article V convention will be a wide-open process, and it is better to accept such situation now and prepare for a slower, more methodical type of convention process where our nearly third of a billion inhabitants have an ability to participate in a meaningful manner. If we leave no one out of deliberations, it will be much more likely that the process will be accepted as legitimate and we as a nation can once again move forward as a leader in innovation, including innovation that returns us to being a democratic republic.

The power to propose amendments in an Article V convention is textually committed to the People, not the state legislatures.[69] The history and intent are clear. By the state legislatures attempting to limit a convention to a specifically worded topic or subject area, the legislatures are invading the People's power to propose amendments. It is time for state legislators to end the practice of requesting limited topic or special interest Article V conventions. State legislatures do not have the power to enforce this. It has become a confusion and a deception. Politicians confuse the public by acting as if they are doing something when the so-called "leaders" know there is almost no likelihood that a state application for a limited topic convention can limit an Article V convention.

State legislators need to shift to calling for a general Article V convention, without limit as to topic or subject matter, and begin thinking what the general Article V convention will look like. Anticipating these problems, I have developed and propose to my fellow Americans some version of a Tricameralism Amendment, as set forth in Chapter 5, as the structure for an Article V convention as well. I am hopeful this will help the American People to begin to think about what needs to be done to correct the flaw in the Article V Convention Clause and to begin a convention.

LIMITS AS TO HOW LONG THE ARTICLE V CONVENTION CAN MEET

Congress may not limit how long an Article V convention can meet. Placing a time limit on the People's deliberations is a power over the People. The terms of the Ninth and Tenth Amendments, combined with their purpose and history, make clear that Congress has no such power. When the People sit in convention, only the People's delegates elected for that specific purpose have the power to vote to conclude the convention.

Our population is one hundred times what it was during the 1787 Convention. Proposing amendments and deliberating will take as long as it takes. We really cannot go the direction of the first Convention, where only a few dozen wealthy, white, Christian men got to call all of the shots. All are entitled to participate in the process, but this time it will be a much slower and methodical process.

If the nation wants to force an end to the Convention, a simple constitutional amendment proposed by Congress and passed by state legislatures acts as a check and balance. The amendment would simply need to indicate that any current Article V convention shall cease activity as of a date certain and that another vote of two-thirds of state legislatures will be required to begin a new Article V convention.

STATE MODIFICATIONS OF CONSTITUTIONAL RULES

One of the most disturbing developments in the state legislatures regarding an Article V convention is the unconstitutional trend to enact legislation making the constitutional standards even higher than those set by the Constitution. In Article V, a supermajority is required to call a convention and to ratify amendments. No such supermajority standard is set forth as to votes within the state legislatures for the call of the convention. In the law, when no supermajority standard is set forth, the standard is assumed to be majority vote. This is even more true when the clause or article itself sets a supermajority standard for certain types of votes but not others, as in Article V.

According to the Congressional Research Service, some states "require that their legislatures approve applications for an Article V convention by the same supermajorities they impose for proposals to amend their own constitutions."[70] Some states may require the legislative vote for a general Article V convention to be as high as 60% to 75%.[71] Article V, however, already sets a supermajority standard, that of two-thirds of the state legislatures needing to vote for the call of the convention and three-quarters of the states needing to ratify a proposed amendment. Adding another layer of supermajority vote requirement alters the balance struck by the nation when the Constitution was ratified. Amending through Article V is already too difficult. The very fact that we have not used our primary check and balance against out of control government is itself evidence that the standard is already too high.

State legislation changing constitutional requirements is unconstitutional. In an analogous situation, in the 1922 case of *Leser v. Garnett*[72], the Supreme Court stated:

> "the function of a state legislature in ratifying a proposed amendment to the federal Constitution, like the function of Congress in proposing the amendment, is a federal function derived from the federal Constitution, and it transcends any limitations sought to be imposed by the people of a state."[73]

Likewise, a state legislative vote for an Article V convention is also a federal function derived from the federal Constitution. A state legislature may not impose a more difficult standard, such as a supermajority vote, than the standards already set forth in the U.S. Constitution.[74]

As the nation moves toward an Article V convention, proponents of the Article V convention will have to watch over their state legislatures. Part of the problem is the confusion surrounding whether states can limit an Article V convention to a limited topic or subject matter. While there is dispute, it appears that Article V does not allow such limits. As to state votes for a general Article V convention, there is no serious argument supporting more layers of supermajority vote than the Constitution already requires.

State legislators are required to take an oath supporting the United States Constitution, including supporting the amendment clause at Article V.[75] Article V provides two paths to amend the U.S. Constitution. One path starts with Congress proposing amendments. The other path starts with the state legislatures voting for an Article V convention. The convention alternative was meant as a check and balance against the national government. A state legislator's oath to support the Constitution includes the duty to keep open and available the peaceful path to amendment meant to protect the People from the national government. When state legislators add another layer of supermajority vote to an already too difficult standard, the state legislators are violating their oaths. They are weakening the rights and interests of the People in the other 49 states to obtain an Article V convention. By making the Article V convention process even more difficult, state legislators are taking the side of the national government over the People. At the very least, they are violating the spirit of their oath, and it reflects both incompetency and corruption at the state level.

Every state legislature should immediately take steps to eliminate any supermajority vote requirement in their state for a general Article V convention. If they do not, we should start voting in only state legislators who promise to advocate for an Article V convention from the perspective of the People, which means making it easier rather than more difficult to obtain the call of the convention. Lawsuits may need to be filed in states which add an unconstitutional layer of supermajority vote, on the ground of being repugnant to the Constitution.

TIMELINESS/CONTEMPORANEITY OF APPLICATIONS

One of the ways Congress has come up with to prevent an Article V convention from occurring is by trying to add requirements that the Constitution does not state. One such ploy is to claim that all applications for an Article V convention must be contemporaneous, or received in the same general time period. This is enlarging Congressional power by enlarging the interpretation of the Constitution, which the Ninth Amendment does not allow.

We can certainly talk at any future Article V convention about "cleaning up" Article V itself. Maybe we want a rule that all Article V applications must be received within a certain number of years. However, this would further limit the People's sovereignty, and might not be a good idea. For now, assume there is no time limit for adding up state votes for a general Article V convention, and begin working toward obtaining 34 state votes for a general Article V convention for proposing constitutional amendments.

WITHDRAWING/RESCINDING/RETRACTING APPLICATIONS AND RATIFICATIONS

There is some dispute about whether state legislatures can withdraw their vote for an Article V convention or withdraw a state's vote for ratification of a proposed amendment. The practice is now common, and is probably constitutional. It is a different situation than adding a supermajority vote requirement. Adding a supermajority requirement upsets the balance already agreed to in the Constitution. Taking one's vote back does not. In the final analysis, these issues should be clarified at the constitutional level through an Article V convention.

CURRENT OFFICEHOLDERS/LEGISLATORS SERVING AS ARTICLE V CONVENTION DELEGATES

Can politicians do double duty, "hold down" two jobs, and collect two salaries by both serving in office and serving as a convention delegate? The U.S. Constitution, at Article I, Section 6, paragraph 2, states: "[N]o Person holding any Office under the United States, shall be a Member of either House during his Continuance in Office.[76] Some scholars dispute whether an Article V delegate is someone who holds an "Office under the United States," and take the position that this clause would not prevent U.S. legislators from serving as delegates to an Article V convention.

Because the convention alternative was meant as a way to get around a corrupt or recalcitrant national legislature, there is a strong argument that members of Congress would be in a conflict of interest, and cannot serve two masters. There is also the practical reality that all of our politicians at the national level are not capable of completing the work that is already on their desks. Why would we want the same incompetent politicians screwing up the People's convention as well? We are talking about our fundamental law. The task deserves the full effort of all participants.

The better rule is probably that a current legislator, at either the state or national level, must resign their legislative position to serve as a delegate to an Article V convention. This may in turn require states with term limits for state office to consider adding more time, as an exception, for any representative or senator who resigned mid-office to serve as a convention delegate. I would expect the rule to allow state office holders to continue in office until the start of the convention, rather than resign before one even knows if they will be voted in as a delegate. Again, these issues should be addressed and uniform rules decided upon, at the first Article V convention, to avoid the confusion of an unclear set of rules.

COURTS AND POLITICAL QUESTIONS

Corrupt politicians and operatives may attempt to deceive the American People into believing that Congress has the power to exclude the Judicial

Branch from hearing any matter regarding an Article V convention, based upon some highly criticized and doubtful language in the 1939 Supreme Court case of *Coleman v. Miller*.[77] Sometimes the Supreme Court takes up a case but issues an opinion that it will not rule in the case because the matter is a "political question." In such cases, the Court generally believes the Constitution does not provide enough direction for the Court to make a ruling. In reality, sometimes the Court will claim a matter is a "political question" when the Court is not sure its ruling will be respected and the Court does not want to damage its power or respect within our three-branch system.

The political question doctrine has been refined over the years. In the 1962 case of *Baker v. Carr*[78], the Supreme Court set forth these elements to review in determining whether an issue is a political question:

1. "A textually demonstrable constitutional commitment of the issue to a coordinate political department"[79]; or
2. "a lack of judicially discoverable and manageable standards for resolving it"[80]; or
3. "[A] series of quasi-prudential considerations of deference to political branches and avoidance of judicial policymaking,"[81] including:
   A. "the impossibility of deciding without an initial policy determination of a kind clearly for nonjudicial discretion; or"[82]
   B. "the impossibility of a court's undertaking independent resolution without expressing lack of the respect due coordinate branches of government; or"[83]
   C. "an unusual need for unquestioning adherence to a political decision already made; or"[84]
   D. "the potentiality of embarrassment from multifarious pronouncements by various departments on one question."[85]

The vast majority of issues surrounding Article V jurisprudence will not be political questions.[86] The first element is not met, because proposing amendments by the convention alternative is not a power committed by the Constitution to Congress[87], but to the People via Article V as modi-fied by the Preamble and the 9th, 10th, 14th, 15th, 17th, 19th, 24th, and 26th Amendments. We have a judicially discoverable standard, the standard most consistent with popular sovereignty. A "one person, one vote" rule, and a rule requiring that the People elect convention delegates are the obvious standards for voting. There really is not any issue of the Court showing disrespect for the other branches.

The real question will be whether members of the Supreme Court have also become so corrupt that they rule in favor of the government and show disrespect to the concept of sovereignty by the People. I do not think the Court is that corrupt, the problem with the Court is how Justices are approved by a corrupted legislative system no longer connected with the People. If Article V convention issues are brought before the Supreme Court, I predict we will see unanimous opinions from the Court on issues like "one person, one vote" and election of convention delegates by the People.

STATE RATIFICATION CONVENTIONS

Article V speaks of two types of conventions, the Article V convention itself and the state ratification conventions as an optional mode of ratifica-tion. Another problem we will have to face is that many of our state legis-lators appear to be oblivious of their duty to protect the peaceful pathway to amendment through Article V. It is possible that the country may need to amend quickly, due to tyranny ramping up quickly. In such a case, we would want our state legislatures to already have set up the rules and pro-cedures for any required ratification convention under Article V.

Some states, however, apparently do not have any procedures for a convention.[88] Such procedures should be agreed upon within each state in advance, when events do not cause there to be a premium on obstructive behavior. States with existing procedures for a consti-tutional convention need to review such legislation and ensure it is appropriate and within constitutional parameters for an Article V state ratification convention.

MOST REMAINING ISSUES SHOULD BE HANDLED BY THE ARTICLE V CONVENTION ITSELF

Establishing the rules and procedure for the Article V convention is for the delegates who have been elected by the People to decide. These issues include:

* voting percentage required for a proposed amendment to be sent to Congress for choice of mode of ratification and to the states for ratification;
* motion rules, including the percentage vote required to bring a proposal to the floor for debate and deliberation and how voting will be conducted, within Constitutional limits;
* who will chair the proceedings;
* whether proceedings can go into private session, and how often do the convention delegates need to report to the public;
* how long the convention will last;
* how long proposed amendments will remain live and active for ratification.

Because of our diversity, at least the first part of the Article V convention, when the rules and procedures are established, should involve broad participation of the American People, with robust, ample representation along the lines set forth in The Tricameralism Amendment introduced in Chapter 5. With respect to the method of choosing delegates and how many delegates will attend, the state legislatures need to coordinate relatively non-controversial rules for beginning the convention. The state legislatures do not actually have the power to impose these rules, so the agreed rules will have to be a "suggestion" to the convention delegates, subject to change once the convention begins.[89]

CHAPTER 10

American Exceptionalism

*"A Republic may be converted into an aristocracy or oligarchy
as well by limiting the number capable of being elected . . ."*[1]

(JAMES MADISON, AT CONVENTION, AUGUST 10, 1787)

SLOWLY, <u>OVER THE COURSE OF time</u>, our nation has morphed from being a republic to being somewhat of a mix of aristocracy and oligarchy. Politicians have essentially converted our republic by limiting the number elected by refusing to increase representatives as the population has increased. By politicians failing to make adjustments to our representation system to account for rapid human population growth, we have slowly lost the republican nature of, and our connection to, the Founding Generation's government. Because Congress will not act, we have only one peaceful path to correct matters – an Article V convention to propose constitutional amendments.

The bad news is we really do not have a right to alter our Constitution via Article V because the Convention Clause is defective, without express rules of representation. The good news is we are now wide open to choose a representation system for a convention that corrects for the gradual erosion of the foundations of our check and balance system.

My advice to my fellow Americans is that we take the strongest possible position on behalf of the concepts of "We the People" and

popular sovereignty as we enter into public negotiations regarding the initial default representational rules for the First Article V Convention of the United States of America.

For the Article V convention to work properly, we must all demand and insure that it will be the People that elect delegates to all conventions. We must oppose all attempts by state legislatures to take from us the right to choose our delegates. By using the proposed third legislative division in the tricameral structure set forth in Chapter 5 as a means to begin the First Article V Convention, we set up a type of structure which more closely satisfies the intended guidelines of the originally proposed Bill of Rights, with all twelve of the proposed amendments.

The third division in the tricameral structure will serve as a substitute Size of Congress Amendment, adapted to account for our substantial human population increase since 1800 (see Graph 1: *World Population, 1300-2000*, at page 25.) These will basically be ad-hoc rules committees that meet to agree to the voting and motion rules and procedures for the convention. By starting with a low-key approach, we can start the First Article V convention as more of a Constitution Project, where all Americans get to participate and give some feedback, at least for the first part of the Convention, when the rules are being set up. This will allow us to get the added tricameral structure working and gain the trust and acceptance of the American People. **We cannot turn over this responsibility to the two political parties.** Part of the reason we need to call for an Article V convention is the failure of the parties, for over 100 years, to protect the People's foundation, our right to a meaningful representative and our right and power to alter our form of government. The two dominant political parties in America are corrupt.

Initially, the most important thing to do to get the new system working, where people will see the improvement and gain confidence in the newly proposed system, is to set up a new communication network to each new subdistrict. Allow all of the public to comment on the rules and procedures. Encourage public comments to be made to each person's sub-representative. The sub-representatives of the Constitutional Enclaves can then see the bigger picture of the needs and inspirations of the people in their district. The thirty sub-representatives in each district will consolidate all of the information coming in from the various parts of the district, and make sure all interests in the district have a voice.

Over time, the system should work much more efficiently, especially if thirty-eight state legislatures go along with the proposal of giving the third division of Congress, the Constitutional Enclaves, the power to replace each District's representative with one of the thirty district sub-representatives. Combining this Power to Replace with the Power to Propose Amendments, as a type of hybrid Article V convention and third division of Congress, is in my opinion at this time the strongest position the American People can take on behalf of ourselves to shore up the foundations of our constitutional check and balance system. As referenced in Chapter 1, we fix two related problems (1. meaningful representation, 2. clear amendment process) with one additional structure, like shooting two apples with one arrow.

I propose that the third division of the tricameral structure be adopted as a skeletal model to start off the First Article V Convention, subject to the structure being changed at the public's demand or the delegates' discretion. However, I believe that as long as we are in what I have referred to as a type of permanent "war time constitution," with the Bill of Rights generally weakened at the constitutional level, we should keep an Article V convention open until such time as we go back to "peace time constitution." The fact is, we may never go back to "peace time constitution." The combination of factors of continued increasing human population, the advent of the digital, connected world, huge inequalities in human wealth and dignity, and the advent of violent terrorist death cults bent on our destruction argue in favor of the type of hybrid system I am proposing. Such would act as an appropriate check and balance for factors that the Framers and Ratifiers could never have anticipated in the Founding period. With a robust committee system, the third division of the tricameral legislative system should serve our needs as both the initial Article V convention rule making body and the amendment proposing body as well.

I am also hoping that we will employ more sense as to who we elect to be a delegate to any Article V convention. This is not a "throat cutter" exercise. This is a time for the more thoughtful among us. We will want to insist on a more courteous and diplomatic leadership than that to which we have become accustomed under the so-called "leadership" of the two corporate political parties.

It would be the height of ignorance to wait to move toward an Article V convention. It could take our nation a decade or more to fight through the various rules and procedural issues before we can even begin the convention. By then, our nation could be in civil war or in a full-fledged totalitarian system.

The concept of **American Exceptionalism** is based upon **two core concepts**, with one more predominant. The dominant concept of American Exceptionalism is based upon our nation introducing **the concept of popular sovereignty** (see Chapter 9) to the world. We honor our Founding Generation due to their character and wisdom to create such a system rather than pursue power for themselves.

American Exceptionalism is also based upon two related concepts from the Christian Bible which guided the behavior of the Framers:

Matthew 5:25: "Agree with thine adversary quickly, while thou art in the way with him."

Matthew 20:27: "And whosoever will be chief among you, let him be your servant."

This brings us full circle to the concept of virtue discussed in the Introduction to this book. Service to and compromise for the greater good are the core concepts of virtue.

When you choose your delegate to the Article V convention, choose individuals who are dedicated to preserving the People's sovereignty, and committed to do so in the spirit of compromise and service to one another. We want representatives who know that their function is to work toward the common good, which means a duty to meet and consult with the delegates from other parts of the country and listen to the various ideas presented on how to improve the Constitution or any proposed amendment thereto.   It is essential that our delegates come to the convention open to being persuaded to the best solution for the entirety of the country.

By returning our nation to a republic with a more sound foundational footing in meaningful representation and a clear process for amendment, we lead the rest of the world by example. **In this manner, the United States of America will regain its undeniable position as the exceptional leader in the free world.**

How To Proceed

Immediately begin to demand and instruct your senator and representative in your state's legislature to bring to the floor and approve a motion for a general convention for proposing constitutional amendments, pursuant to Article V of the United States Constitution. We need to teach our own state politicians that they must protect the peaceful path of an Article V convention. Many legislators have no clue that Article V is defective, largely because we have not used it. They must be taught.

If the current batch of state legislators will not act to protect our interests and liberties, then the battle is on. Each state election, find someone to run on an Article V convention platform. Vote only for leaders who have the courage to stand up and teach these important and valuable lessons:

1. **The Bill of Rights was never completed.** The Framers intended 12 amendments, but only 10 were initially passed, with the eleventh now our Twenty-Seventh Amendment. The originally proposed first amendment was initially intended to limit each member of the House of Representatives to representing no more than 50,000 to 60,000 people. This Article V movement is a Convention of the People movement, not a Convention of the States movement. We seek to correct constitutional errors based on the lessons of experience, not raw belief or philosophy, and return our government to republican principles. We fight for meaningful representation.

2. **The Article V Convention Clause is defective** because the method of choosing delegates and the voting rules are not in place. The Convention Clause is one of the most important check and balances in the Constitution, as it allows us a peaceful means to both correct errors learned by experience and make necessary changes when Congress becomes corrupt or will not act. We fight to reestablish the People's right and power to alter the form of our government by ensuring clear and meaningful representational rules for an Article V convention.

If you wish, you may write in the following manner, or just copy the sample letter, sign it and send it to your state legislators:

SAMPLE LETTER TO STATE LEGISLATOR

Dear Congressperson:

We the People, of the United States of America, hereby demand and instruct you to immediately take all necessary steps to bring to the floor of your assembly, and secure the votes for approval, **a motion for a general convention for proposing constitutional amendments under Article V of the United States Constitution**.

We the People demand that the First Article V Convention propose an appropriate amendment and reformation to the Article V Convention Clause, which was clearly intended by the Founding Generation to provide the People a peaceful and lawful means, without the consent of the United States Congress, to make and alter our constitutions of government.

That right and power is in fact **not secured.** The convention right referred to in Article V is illusory, as there is no express remedy to choose the delegates to begin an Article V convention. This single right and power, to make and alter our form of government, is the entire basis for a democratic republic. If not secured, the error in Article V allows the public mischief of public claims that without a means for the People to alter their Constitution and form of government, the underlying ethical obligation to follow the laws does not exist.

The error in the Article V Convention Clause is well known, learned through experience. A good place to begin learning about the problem and a solution is in the book by Daniel J. Tekunoff, Guide to the First Article V Convention of the People. Please coordinate with other state legislatures in agreeing to a broad based and robust representational structure for the beginning of the First Article V Convention, when the rules and procedures for the Convention will need to be set up.

From this point forward, We the People intend to vote only for state legislative candidates who promise to move, vote and gain approval for this state's demand and application for a convention for the purpose of proposing amendments to the United States Constitution, pursuant to Article V thereof. If you are not on board with the interests of shoring up the People's Article V Convention power and right, by ensuring clear rules for choosing the People's representatives required to start the convention, our intention is to work for your removal and replacement with someone who is.

Thank you, Congressperson, and here is to the hope that you will take the People's interests and liberties to heart.

Yours very truly,

SAMPLE TEXT FOR STATE LEGISLATORS:

Article V uses a formal term of art – APPLICATION – to basically mean a state legislature's notice to Congress that such state legislature has voted in favor of beginning an Article V convention for the general purpose of proposing amendments to the U.S. Constitution.

Article V provides for a convention for the general purpose of generally proposing amendments, not for a limited purpose of proposing a single amendment or proposing amendments in a limited subject matter area.

CORE TEXT FOR STATE LEGISLATOR'S MOTION FOR THAT STATE LEGISLATURE'S VOTE FOR AN ARTICLE V CONVENTION

Motion Sample:
Motion is hereby made that The Legislature of the State of_____, a member of this United States of America, vote in favor of a general Article V Convention to propose Amendments to the United States Constitution, pursuant to Article V of the United States Constitution, and that this Legislature further deliver to the United States Congress appropriate notice and Application of this State Legislature's vote for a general Convention to propose Amendments to said Constitution, pursuant to said Article V.

CORE TEXT FOR STATE LEGISLATIVE NOTICE TO CONGRESS OF STATE LEGISLATURE'S VOTE FOR AN ARTICLE V CONVENTION

Language to be sent to United States Congress (either sample can be used)

Sample 1:
The Legislature of the State of _____ hereby delivers to the United States Congress this APPLICATION for a Convention to propose Amendments to said United States Constitution, pursuant to said Article V.

Sample 2:

The Legislature of the State of _____hereby delivers to the United States Congress this APPLICATION for a general Convention to propose Amendments to said United States Constitution, pursuant to said Article V.

The Documentary Record of the Bill of Rights' Passage Through the First Congress of The United States of America

Please consider and compare the following four versions of the Bill of Rights, reflecting the actual documentary evidence of the evolution of the language of the Bill of Rights before being presented to the people and ratified by the state legislatures.

AMENDMENTS PASSED BY THE HOUSE OF REPRESENTATIVES
August 24, 1789[1]

ARTICLE THE FIRST

After the first enumeration, required by the first Article of the Constitution, there shall be one Representative for every thirty thousand until the number shall amount to one hundred after which the proportion shall be so regulated by Congress that there shall be not less than one hundred Representatives nor less than one Representative for every forty thousand persons, until the number of representatives shall amount to two hundred after which the proportion shall be so regulated by Congress, that there shall not be less than two hundred Representatives, nor less than one Representative for every fifty thousand persons.

ARTICLE THE SECOND

No law varying the compensation to the members of Congress, shall take effect, until an election of Representatives shall have intervened.

ARTICLE THE THIRD

Congress shall make no law establishing religion or prohibiting the free exercise thereof, nor shall the rights of Conscience be infringed.

ARTICLE THE FOURTH

The Freedom of Speech, and of the Press, and the right of the people peaceably to assemble, and consult for their common good, and to apply to the Government for a redress of grievances, shall not be infringed.

ARTICLE THE FIFTH

A well regulated militia, composed of the body of the People, being the best security of a free State, the right of the People to keep and bear arms shall not be infringed but no one religiously scrupulous of bearing arms, shall be compelled to render military service in person.

ARTICLE THE SIXTH

No soldier shall, in time of peace, be quartered in any house without the consent of the owner, or in time of war but in a manner to be prescribed by law.

ARTICLE THE SEVENTH

The right of the people to be secure in their persons, houses, papers and effects, against unreasonable searches and seizures, shall not be violated, and no warrants shall issue but upon probable cause supported by oath or affirmation, and particularly describing the place to be searched, and the persons or things to be seized.

ARTICLE THE EIGHTH

No person shall be subject, except in case of impeachment, to more than one trial, or one punishment for the same offense, nor shall be compelled in any criminal case, to be a witness against himself, nor be deprived of life, liberty or property without due process of law; nor shall private property be taken for public use without just compensation.

ARTICLE THE NINTH

In all criminal prosecutions, the accused shall enjoy the right to a speedy and public trial, to be informed of the nature and cause of the accusation to be confronted with the witnesses against him, to have compulsory process for obtaining witnesses in his favor and to have the assistance of counsel for his defence.

ARTICLE THE TENTH

The trial of all crimes (except in case of impeachment, and in cases arising in the land or naval forces, or in the militia when in actual service in time of War or public danger) shall be by an impartial Jury of the Vicinage with the requisite of unanimity for conviction, the right of challenge and other accostomed requisites; and no person shall be held to answer for a capital, or otherways infamous crime, unless on a presentment or indictment by a Grand Jury; but if a crime be committed in a place in the possession of an enemy, or in which an insurrection may prevail, the indictment and trial may by law be authorised in some other place within the same State.

ARTICLE THE ELEVENTH

No appeal to the Supreme Court of the United States, shall be allowed, where the value in controversy shall not amount to one thousand dollars nor shall any fact triable by a Jury according to the course of the common law, be otherwise re-examinable, than according to the rules of common law.

ARTICLE THE TWELFTH

In suits at common law, the right of trial by jury shall be preserved.

ARTICLE THE THIRTEENTH

Excessive bail shall not be required, nor excessive fines imposed, nor cruel and unusual punishments inflicted.

ARTICLE THE FOURTEENTH

No state shall infringe the right of trial by Jury in criminal cases, nor the rights of conscience, nor the freedom of speech, or of the press.

ARTICLE THE FIFTEENTH

The enumeration in the Constitution of certain rights, shall not be construed to deny or disparage others retained by the people.

ARTICLE THE SIXTEENTH

The powers delegated by the Constitution to the government of the United States, shall be exercised as therein appropriated, so that the Legislative shall never exercise the powers vested in the Executive or Judicial; nor the Executive the powers vested in the Legislative or Judicial; nor the Judicial the powers vested in the Legislative or Executive.

ARTICLE THE SEVENTEENTH

The powers not delegated by the Constitution, nor prohibited by it, to the States, are reserved to the States respectively.

AMENDMENTS PASSED BY THE SENATE
September 9, 1789[2]

ARTICLE THE FIRST
After the first enumeration, required by the first article of the Constitution, there shall be one Representative for every thirty thousand, until the number shall amount to one hundred; to which number one Representative shall be added for every subsequent increase of forty thousand, until the Representatives shall amount to two hundred, to which number one Representative shall be added for every subsequent increase of sixty thousand persons.

ARTICLE THE SECOND
No law, varying the compensation for the services of the Senators and Representatives, shall take effect, until an election of Representatives shall have intervened.

ARTICLE THE THIRD
Congress shall make no law establishing articles of faith, or a mode of worship, or prohibiting the free exercise of religion, or abridging the freedom of speech, or of the press, or the right of the people peaceably to assemble, and to petition to the government for a redress of grievances.

ARTICLE THE FOURTH
A well regulated militia, being necessary to the security of a free State, the right of the people to keep and bear arms, shall not be infringed.

ARTICLE THE FIFTH
No soldier shall, in time of peace, be quartered in any house, without the consent of the owner, nor in time of war, but in a manner to be prescribed by law.

ARTICLE THE SIXTH
The right of the people to be secure in their persons, houses, papers, and effects, against unreasonable searches and seizures, shall not be violated,

and no warrants shall issue, but upon probable cause, supported by oath or affirmation, and particularly describing the place to be searched, and the persons or things to be seized.

ARTICLE THE SEVENTH

No person shall be held to answer for a capital, or otherwise infamous crime, unless on a presentment or indictment of a Grand Jury, except in cases arising in the land or naval forces, or in the militia, when in actual service in time of war or public danger; nor shall any person be subject for the same offence to be twice put in jeopardy of life or limb; nor shall be compelled in any criminal case, to be a witness against himself, nor be deprived of life, liberty or property, without due process of law; nor shall private property be taken for public use without just compensation.

ARTICLE THE EIGHTH

In all criminal prosecutions, the accused shall enjoy the right to a speedy and public trial, to be informed of the nature and cause of the accusation, to be confronted with the witnesses against him, to have compulsory process for obtaining witnesses in his favour, and to have the assistance of counsel for his defence.

ARTICLE THE NINTH

In suits at common law, where the value in controversy shall exceed twenty dollars, the right of trial by Jury shall be preserved, and no fact, tried by a Jury, shall be otherwise re-examined in any court of the United States, than according to the rules of the common law.

ARTICLE THE TENTH

Excessive bail shall not be required, nor excessive fines imposed, nor cruel and unusual punishments inflicted.

ARTICLE THE ELEVENTH

The enumeration in the Constitution of certain rights, shall not be construed to deny or disparage others retained by the people.

ARTICLE THE TWELFTH

The powers not delegated to the United States by the Constitution, nor prohibited by it to the States, are reserved to the States respectively, or to the people.

PROPOSED AMENDMENTS PASSED BY CONGRESS
September 25, 1789[3]

ARTICLE THE FIRST

After the first enumeration required by the first Article of the Constitution, there shall be one Representative for every thirty thousand, until the number shall amount to one hundred, after which, the proportion shall be so regulated by Congress, that there shall be not less than one hundred Representatives, nor less than one Representative for every forty thousand persons, until the number of Representatives shall amount to two hundred, after which the proportion shall be so regulated by Congress, that there shall not be less than two hundred Representatives, nor more than one Representative for every fifty thousand persons.

ARTICLE THE SECOND

No law, varying the compensation for the services of the Senators and Representatives, shall take effect, until an election of Representatives shall have intervened.[4]

ARTICLE THE THIRD

Congress shall make no law respecting an establishment of religion, or prohibiting the free exercise thereof, or abridging the freedom of speech, or of the press, or the right of the people peaceably to assemble, and to petition to the government for a redress of grievances.

ARTICLE THE FOURTH

A well regulated militia, being necessary to the security of a free State, the right of the people to keep and bear arms, shall not be infringed.

ARTICLE THE FIFTH

No soldier shall, in time of peace, be quartered in any house, without the consent of the owner, nor in time of war, but in a manner to be prescribed by law.

ARTICLE THE SIXTH

The right of the people to be secure in their persons, houses, papers, and effects, against unreasonable searches and seizures, shall not be violated, and no warrants shall issue, but upon probable cause, supported by oath or affirmation, and particularly describing the place to be searched and the persons or things to be seized.

ARTICLE THE SEVENTH

No person shall be held to answer for a capital, or otherwise infamous crime, unless on a presentment or indictment of a Grand Jury, except in cases arising in the land or naval forces, or in the militia, when in actual service in time of war or public danger; nor shall any person be subject for the same offence to be twice put in jeopardy of life or limb; nor shall be compelled in any criminal case to be a witness against himself, nor be deprived of life, liberty or property, without due process of law; nor shall private property be taken for public use without just compensation.

ARTICLE THE EIGHTH

In all criminal prosecutions, the accused shall enjoy the right to a speedy and public trial, by an impartial jury of the State and district wherein the crime shall have been committed; which district shall have been previously ascertained by law, and to be informed of the nature and cause of the accusation; to be confronted with the witnesses against him; to have compulsory process for obtaining witnesses in his favour, and to have the assistance of counsel for his defence.

ARTICLE THE NINTH

In suits at common law, where the value in controversy shall exceed twenty dollars, the right of trial by Jury shall be preserved, and no fact tried by a Jury, shall be otherwise re-examined in any Court of the United States, than according to the rules of the common law.

ARTICLE THE TENTH

Excessive bail shall not be required, nor excessive fines imposed, nor cruel and unusual punishments inflicted.

ARTICLE THE ELEVENTH

The enumeration in the Constitution, of certain rights, shall not be construed to deny or disparage others retained by the people.

ARTICLE THE TWELFTH

The powers not delegated to the United States by the Constitution, nor prohibited by it to the States, are reserved to the States respectively, or to the people.

THE BILL OF RIGHTS
Ratified by three-quarters of states on December 15, 1791[5]

Amendment I
[Freedom of Religion, Speech and Press; Peaceful Assembly; Petition of Grievances]

Congress shall make no law respecting an establishment of religion, or prohibiting the free exercise thereof; or abridging the freedom of speech, or of the press; or the right of the people peaceably to assemble, and to petition the Government for a redress of grievances.

Amendment II
[Right To Bear Arms]

A well regulated Militia, being necessary to the security of a free State, the right of the people to keep and bear Arms, shall not be infringed.

Amendment III
[Soldiers Denied Quarter in Homes]

No Soldier shall, in time of peace be quartered in any house, without the consent of the Owner, nor in time of war, but in a manner to be prescribed by law.

Amendment IV
[Search and Seizure; Warrants]

The right of the people to be secure in their persons, houses, papers, and effects, against unreasonable searches and seizures, shall not be violated, and no Warrants shall issue, but upon probable cause, supported by Oath or affirmation, and particularly describing the place to be searched, and the persons or things to be seized.

Amendment V
[Grand Jury Indictment for Capital Crimes; Double Jeopardy; Self-Incrimination; Due Process of Law; Just Compensation for Property]

No person shall be held to answer for a capital, or otherwise infamous crime, unless on a presentment or indictment of a Grand Jury, except in cases arising in the land or naval forces, or in the Militia, when in actual service in time of War or public danger; nor shall any person be subject for the same offence to be twice put in jeopardy of life or limb; nor shall be compelled in any criminal case to be a witness against himself, nor be deprived of life, liberty, or property, without due process of law; nor shall private property be taken for public use, without just compensation.

Amendment VI
[Jury trials for crimes, and procedural rights]

In all criminal prosecutions, the accused shall enjoy the right to a speedy and public trial, by an impartial jury of the State and district wherein the crime shall have been committed, which district shall have been previously ascertained by law, and to be informed of the nature and cause of the accusation; to be confronted with the witnesses against him; to have compulsory process for obtaining witnesses in his favor, and to have the Assistance of Counsel for his defence.

Amendment VII
[Civil Trials]

In Suits at common law, where the value in controversy shall exceed twenty dollars, the right of trial by jury shall be preserved, and no fact tried by a jury, shall be otherwise reexamined in any Court of the United States, than according to the rules of the common law.

Amendment VIII
[Excessive Bail, Fines, Punishments]

Excessive bail shall not be required, nor excessive fines imposed, nor cruel and unusual punishments inflicted.

Amendment IX
[The People Retain Power]

The enumeration in the Constitution, of certain rights, shall not be construed to deny or disparage others retained by the people.

Amendment X
[Powers Reserved to States and People]

The powers not delegated to the United States by the Constitution, nor prohibited by it to the States, are reserved to the States respectively, or to the people.

Evolution of Language of Original Proposed First Amendment Limiting How Many People Each Member of House of Representatives May Represent

<u>February 6, 1788</u>, proposed by Massachusetts Convention
That there shall be one representative to every thirty thousand persons according to the Census mentioned in the Constitution until the whole number of the Representatives amounts to Two hundred.

<u>June 21, 1788</u>, proposed by the New Hampshire Convention
That there shall be one Representative to every Thirty thousand Persons according to the Census mentioned in the Constitution until the whole number of the Representatives amounts to Two hundred.

<u>June 27, 1788</u>, proposed by the Virginia Convention
That there shall be one representative for every thirty thousand, according to the Enumeration or Census mentioned in the Constitution, until the whole number of representatives amounts to two hundred; after which that number shall be continued or encreased [sic] as the Congress shall direct, upon the principles fixed by the Constitution by apportioning the Representatives of each State to some greater number of people from time to time as population encreases [sic].

July 26, 1788, proposed by the New York Convention
That there shall be one Representative for ever thirty thousand
Inhabitants, according to the enumeration or Census mentioned in the
Constitution, until the whole number of Representatives amounts to two
hundred; after which that number shall be continued or encreased [sic]
but not diminished, as Congress shall direct, and according to such ration
as the Congress shall fix, in conformity to the rule prescribed for the
Apportionment of Representatives and direct Taxes.

June 8, 1789, Madison's Rough Draft Proposal to First Congress
After the first actual enumeration, there shall be one representative for
every thirty thousand, until the number shall amount to after which the
proportion shall be so regulated by Congress, that the number shall never
be less than nor more than but each state shall after the first enumeration,
have at least two representatives, and prior thereto.

August 24, 1789, House of Representatives First Version of Proposed First
Amendment
After the first enumeration, required by the first Article of the Constitution, there shall be one Representative for every thirty thousand until the
number shall amount to one hundred after which the proportion shall be
so regulated by Congress that there shall be not less than one hundred
Representatives nor less than one Representative for every forty thousand
persons, until the number of representatives shall amount to two hundred
after which the proportion shall be so regulated by Congress, that there
shall not be less than two hundred Representatives, nor less than one Representative for every fifty thousand persons.

September 9, 1789, Senate's Revised Version
After the first enumeration, required by the first article of the Constitution, there shall be one Representative for every thirty thousand, until the

number shall amount to one hundred; to which number one Representative shall be added for every subsequent increase of forty thousand, until the Representatives shall amount to two hundred, to which number <u>one Representative shall be added for every subsequent increase of sixty thousand persons</u>.

<u>September 25, 1789</u>, Final Version Sent to States
After the first enumeration required by the first Article of the Constitution, there shall be one Representative for every thirty thousand, until the number shall amount to one hundred, after which, the proportion shall be so regulated by Congress, that there shall be not less than one hundred Representatives, nor less than one Representative for every forty thousand persons, until the number of Representatives shall amount to two hundred, after which the proportion shall be so regulated by Congress, that there shall not be less than two hundred Representatives, <u>nor more than one Representative for every fifty thousand persons</u>.

Source: Helen E. Veit; Kenneth R. Bowling; Charlene Bangs Bickford (eds.), <u>Creating The Bill of Rights</u>, at pp. 3, 9-12, 14, 16, 19, 25, 37, 46 and 48, The Johns Hopkins University Press, Baltimore, Maryland (1991).

APPENDIX 3

Article V Revision History During Constitutional Convention

[Note: James Madison's notes are the most detailed record, generally, from the Constitutional Convention of 1787. There is also an official Journal and more limited notes of other delegates. Here, Madison's notes are set forth first, with any other convention notes on the topic of amendment on that date set forth beneath Madison's notes for comparison purposes. Bolded portions focus the reader on those portions of the record which discuss the topic of a constitutional convention.]

<u>May 29, 1787</u>
Resolution 13 of The Virginia Plan introduced:
"Resolved that provision ought to be made for the amendment of the Articles of Union whensoever it shall seem necessary, and that the assent of the National Legislature ought not to be required thereto."

<u>June 5, 1787</u>
Madison's notes:
"Mr. Pinkney doubted the propriety or necessity of it.

Mr. Gerry favored it. The novelty & difficulty of the experiment requires periodical revision. The prospect of such a revision would also give intermediate stability to the Govt. Nothing had yet happened in the States where this provision existed to prove its impropriety. – The Proposition was postponed for further consideration."

Journal

It was then moved and seconded to postpone the consideration of the 13th resolution submitted by Mr Randolph

and on the question to postpone

it passed in the affirmative

Yates' Notes

The 13th and 14th resolves postponed.

June 11, 1787

Madison's notes:

"<Resolution 13> for amending the national Constitution hereafter without consent of Natl. Legislature <being> considered, several members did not see the necessity of the <Resolution> at all, nor the propriety of making the consent of the Natl. Legisl. unnecessary.

Col. Mason urged the necessity of such a provision. The plan now to be formed will certainly be defective, as the Confederation has been found on trial to be. Amendments therefore will be necessary, and **it will be better to provide for them, in an easy, regular and Constitutional way than to trust to chance and violence. It would be improper to require the consent of the Natl. Legislature, because they may abuse their power, and refuse their consent on that very account. The opportunity for such an abuse, may be the fault of the Constitution calling for amendment.**

Mr. Randolph <enforced> these arguments.

The words, "without requiring the consent of the Natl. Legislature" were postponed. The other provision in the clause passed nem. con." ["nem. con." means without opposition]

Journal

It was then moved and seconded to agree to the following resolution

Resolved that provision ought to be made for the amendment of the articles of union whensoever it shall seem necessary.

On the question to agree to the same

it passed in the affirmative

It was agreed to postpone the following clause in the 13th resolution submitted by Mr Randolph namely

"and that the assent of the national legislature ought not to be required thereto"

Yates' Notes

13th Resolve – the first part agreed to.

June 13, 1787

Report of the Committee of Whole on Mr. Randolphs propositions

17. [Resolved] that provision ought to be made for the amendment of the Articles of Union whensoever it shall seem necessary.

July 23, 1787

Madison's Notes

Resoln: 17. that provision ought to be made for future amendments of the articles of Union. Agreed to nem con.

Journal

On the question to agree to the 17th resolution, as reported from the Committee of the whole House, namely "That provision ought to be made for the amendment of "the articles of union, whensoever it shall seem necessary" it passed unanimously in the affirmative.

July 26 - August 4, 1787

Committee of Detail change #1:

"An alteration may be effected in the articles of union, on application of two thirds of the state legislatures to the Natl. Leg. they call a Convn. to revise or alter ye Articles of Union."

Committee of Detail change #2:
"This Constitution ought to be amended whenever such Amendment shall become necessary; and on the Application of the Legislatures of two thirds of the States in the Union, the Legislature of the United States shall call a Convention for that Purpose."

August 6, 1787
Committee of Detail report:
"On the application of the Legislatures of two thirds of the States in the Union, for an amendment of this Constitution, the Legislature of the United States shall call a Convention for that purpose."

August 30, 1787
Madison's notes:

> "Art: XIX taken up.
>   Mr. Govr. Morris suggested that the Legislature should be left at liberty to call a Convention, whenever they please.
>   The art: was agreed to nem: con:"

Journal
On the question to agree to the 19 article as reported
it passed in the affirmative

September 5, 1787
Madison's Notes
Mr. Gerry gave notice that he should move to reconsider articles XIX. XX. XXI. XXII.

September 10, 1787
Madison's notes:
Mr Gerry moved to reconsider art XIX. viz, "On the application of the Legislatures of two thirds of the States in the Union, for an amendment of

this Constitution, the Legislature of the U.S. shall call a Convention for that purpose." (see Aug." 6.)

This Constitution he said is to be paramount to the State Constitutions. It follows, hence, from this article that two thirds of the States may obtain a Convention, a majority of which can bind the Union to innovations that may subvert the State-Constitutions altogether. He asked whether this was a situation proper to be run into--

Mr. Hamilton 2ded. the motion, but he said with a different view from Mr. Gerry-- He did not object to the consequences stated by Mr. Gerry-- There was no greater evil in subjecting the people of the U. S. to the major voice than the people of a particular State- It had been wished by many and was much to have been desired that an easier mode for introducing amendments had been provided by the articles of Confederation. It was equally desirable now that an easy mode should be established for supplying defects which will probably appear in the new System. The mode proposed was not adequate. The State Legislatures will not apply for alterations but with a view to increase their own powers-- The National Legislature will be the first to perceive and will be most sensible to the necessity of amendments, and ought also to be empowered, whenever two thirds of each branch should concur to call a Convention-- There could be no danger in giving this power, as the people would finally decide in the case.

Mr Madison remarked on the vagueness of the terms, "call a Convention for the purpose." as sufficient reason for reconsidering the article. How was a Convention to be formed? by what rule decide? what the force of its acts?

On the motion of Mr. Gerry to reconsider . . . [Ayes- 9; noes -- 1; divided- 1.]

Mr. Sherman moved to add to the article "or the Legislature may propose amendments to the several States for their approbation, but no amendments shall be binding until consented to by the several States"

Mr. Gerry 2ded. the motion

Mr. Wilson moved to insert "two thirds of" before the words "several States"--on which amendment to the motion of Mr. Sherman . . . [Ayes--5; noes-- 6.]

Mr. Wilson then moved to insert "three fourths of" before "the several Sts" which was agreed to nem: con:

Mr. Madison moved to postpone the consideration of the amended proposition in order to take up the following,

"The Legislature of the U-- S-- whenever two thirds of both Houses shall deem necessary, or on the application of two thirds of the Legislatures of the several States, shall propose amendments to this Constitution, which shall be valid to all intents and purposes as part thereof, when the same shall have been ratified by three fourths at least of the Legislatures of the several States, or by Conventions in three fourths thereof, as one or the other mode of ratification may be proposed by the Legislature of the U. S:"

Mr. Hamilton 2ded. the motion.

Mr. Rutlidge said he never could agree to give a power by which the articles relating to slaves might be altered by the States not interested in that property and prejudiced against it. In order to obviate this objection, these words were added to the proposition: "* provided that no amendments which may be made prior to the year 1808. shall in any manner affect the 4 & 5 sections of the VII article" -- The postponement being agreed to,

On the question On the proposition of Mr. Madison & Mr. Hamilton as amended . . . [Ayes--9; noes 1; divided -- 1.]

Journal
It was moved and seconded to reconsider the 19th article
which passed in the affirmative [Ayes- 9; noes- 1; divided- 1.]

It was moved and seconded to amend the 19 article by adding the following clause.

Or the Legislature may propose amendments to the several States, for their approbation, but no amendments shall be binding, until consented to by the several States.

It was moved and seconded to insert the words "two thirds of" before the words "the several States"

which passed in the negative [Ayes- 5; noes- 6.]

It was moved and seconded to insert the words "three fourths" which passed in the affirmative. ["unanimous"]

It was moved and seconded to postpone the consideration of the amendment in order to take up the following.

"The Legislature of the United States, whenever two thirds of both Houses shall deem necessary, or on the application of two thirds of the Legislatures of the several States, shall propose amendments to this Constitution which shall be valid to all intents and purposes as part thereof, when the same shall have been ratified by three fourths at least of the Legislatures of the several States, or by Conventions in three fourths thereof, as one or the other mode of ratification may be proposed by the Legislature of the United-States: Provided that no amendments which may be made prior to the year 1808. shall in any manner affect the 4th and 5th Sections of article the 7th

On the question to postpone it passed in the affirmative

On the question to agree to the last amendment.

It passed in the affirmative [Ayes – 9; noes – 1; divided – 1.]

September 12, 1787
Committee of Style report:
The Congress, whenever two-thirds of both houses shall deem necessary, or on the application of two-thirds of the legislatures of the several states, shall propose amendments to this constitution, which shall be valid to all intents and purposes, as part thereof, when the same shall have been ratified by three-fourths at least of the legislatures of the several states, or

by conventions in three-fourths thereof, as the one or the other mode of ratification may be proposed by the Congress: Provided, that no amendment which may be made prior to the year 1808 shall in any manner affect the _____ and _____ sections of article _____

September 15, 1787
Madison's notes:
Art-- V. "The Congress, whenever two thirds of both Houses shall deem necessary, or on the application of two thirds of the Legislatures of the several States shall propose amendments to this Constitution, which shall be valid to all intents and purposes as part thereof, when the same shall have been ratified by three fourths at least of the Legislatures of the several States, or by Conventions in three fourths thereof, as the one or the other mode of ratification may be proposed by the Congress: Provided that no amendment which may be made prior to the year 1808 shall in any manner affect the <1 & 4 clauses in the 9.> section of article I."

Mr. Sherman expressed his fears that three fourths of the States might be brought to do things fatal to particular States, as abolishing them altogether or depriving them of their equality in the Senate. He thought it reasonable that the proviso in favor of the States importing slaves should be extended so as to provide that no State should be affected in its internal police, or deprived of its equality in the Senate.

Col: Mason thought the plan of amending the Constitution exceptionable & dangerous. As the proposing of amendments is in both the modes to depend, in the first immediately, and in the second, ultimately, on Congress, no amendments of the proper kind would ever be obtained by the people, if the Government should become oppressive, as he verily believed would be the case.

Mr. Govr. Morris & Mr. Gerry moved to amend the article so as to require a Convention on application of ⅔ the States

Mr Madison did not see why Congress would not be as much bound to propose amendments applied for by two thirds of the States as to call a call [sic] a Convention on the like application. He saw no

objection however against providing for a Convention for the purpose of amendments, except only that difficulties might arise as to the form, the quorum etc. which in Constitutional regulations ought to be as much as possible avoided.

The motion of Mr. Govr Morris and Mr. Gerry was agreed to nem: con (see: the first part of the article as finally past)

Mr Sherman moved to strike out of art. V. after "legislatures" the words "of three fourths" and so after the word "Conventions" leaving future Conventions to act in this matter, like the present Conventions according to circumstances.

On this motion . . . [Ayes -- 3; noes -- 7; divided -- x.]

Mr Gerry moved to strike out the words "or by Conventions in three fourths thereof" On this motion . . . [Ayes- 1; noes - 10.]

—- Sherman moved according to his idea above expressed to annex to the end of the article a further proviso "that no State shall without its consent be affected in its internal police, or deprived of its equal suffrage in the Senate",

Mr. Madison. Begin with these special provisos, and every State will insist on them, for their boundaries, exports etc.

On the motion of Mr. Sherman . . . [Ayes--3; noes -- 8.]

Mr. Sherman then moved to strike out art V altogether

Mr Brearley 2ded. the motion, on which . . . [Ayes- 2; noes -- 8; divided -- 1.]

Mr. Govr Morris moved to annex a further proviso –"that no State, without its consent shall be deprived of its equal suffrage in the Senate"

This motion being dictated by the circulating murmurs of the small States was agreed to without debate, no one opposing it, or on the question, saying no.

Col: Mason expressing his discontent at the power given to Congress by a bare majority to pass navigation acts, which he said would not only enhance the freight, a consequence he did not so much regard -- but would enable a few rich merchants in Philada N. York & Boston, to monopolize the Staples of the Southern States & reduce their value perhaps 50 Per Ct – moved a further proviso "that no law in nature of a navigation act be passed before the year 1808, without the consent of ⅔ of each branch of the Legislature

On this motion . . . [Ayes--3; noes -- 7; absent -- 1.]

McHenry's Notes
Added to the V article amended "No State without its consent shall be deprived of its equal suffrage in the Senate.

Sources by Date:
May 29, 1787: 1 M. Farrand (ed.), <u>The Records of the Federal Convention of 1787</u>, at pp. 20-22.
June 5, 1787: Id., at pp. 117, 121-122, 126.
June 11, 1787: Id., at pp. 194, 202-203, 206.
June 13, 1787: Id., at p. 237.
July 23, 1787: 2 M. Farrand (ed.), <u>The Records of the Federal Convention of 1787</u>, at pp. 84, 87.
July 26 – August 4, 1787: Id., at pp. 148, 159, 174.
August 6, 1787: Id., at p. 188.
August 30, 1787: Id., at pp. 461, 467-468.
September 5, 1787: Id., at p. 511
September 10, 1787: Id., at pp. 555-559
September 12, 1787: Id., at pp. 590, 602
September 15, 1787: Id., at pp. 629-631, 634.

Additional Notes from the Constitutional Convention Re: The Topic of Constitutional Amendments

June 5, 1787
Journal
It was then moved and seconded to postpone the consideration of the 13th resolution submitted by Mr Randolph
    and on the question to postpone
    it passed in the affirmative

Yates' Notes
The 13th and 14th resolves postponed.

June 11, 1787
Journal
It was then moved and seconded to agree to the following resolution
    Resolved that provision ought to be made for the amendment of the articles of union whensoever it shall seem necessary.
    On the question to agree to the same
    it passed in the affirmative
    It was agreed to postpone the following clause in the 13th resolution submitted by Mr Randolph namely
    "and that the assent of the national legislature ought not to be required thereto"

Yates' Notes
13ᵗʰ Resolve – the first part agreed to.

August 30, 1787
Journal
On the question to agree to the 19 article as reported
it passed in the affirmative

September 10, 1787
Journal
It was moved and seconded to reconsider the 19th article
which passed in the affirmative [Ayes- 9; noes- 1; divided- 1.]
It was moved and seconded to amend the 19 article by adding the following clause.
Or the Legislature may propose amendments to the several States, for their approbation, but no amendments shall be binding, until consented to by the several States.
It was moved and seconded to insert the words "two thirds of" before the words "the several States"
which passed in the negative [Ayes- 5; noes- 6.]
It was moved and seconded to insert the words "three fourths" which passed in the affirmative. ["unanimous"]
It was moved and seconded to postpone the consideration of the amendment in order to take up the following.
"The Legislature of the United States, whenever two thirds of both Houses shall deem necessary, or on the application of two thirds of the Legislatures of the several States, shall propose amendments to this Constitution which shall be valid to all intents and purposes as part thereof, when the same shall have been ratified by three fourths at least of the Legislatures of the several States, or by Conventions in three fourths thereof, as one or the other mode of ratification may be proposed by the Legislature of the United-States: Provided that no amendments which may be made prior to

the year 1808. shall in any manner affect the 4th and 5th Sections of article the 7th

On the question to postpone it passed in the affirmative
On the question to agree to the last amendment.
It passed in the affirmative [Ayes – 9; noes – 1; divided – 1.]

September 15, 1787
McHenry's Notes
Added to the V article amended "No State without its consent shall be deprived of its equal suffrage in the Senate.

The Constitution of the United States of America

WE THE PEOPLE OF THE **United States**, in Order to form a more perfect Union, establish Justice, insure domestic Tranquility, provide for the common defence, promote the general Welfare, and secure the Blessings of Liberty to ourselves and our Posterity, **do ordain and establish this CONSTITUTION for the United States of America.**

Article 1
[THE LEGISLATIVE BRANCH]

Section 1 [Legislative powers vested in Congress]
All legislative Powers herein granted shall be vested in a Congress of the United States, which shall consist of a Senate and House of Representatives.

Section 2 [House of Representatives]

[1] The House of Representatives shall be composed of Members chosen every second Year by the People of the several States, and the Electors in each State shall have the Qualifications requisite for Electors of the most numerous Branch of the State Legislature.

[2] No Person shall be a Representative who shall not have attained to the Age of twenty five Years, and been seven Years a Citizen of the United States, and who shall not, when elected, be an Inhabitant of that State in which he shall be chosen.

[3] Representatives and direct Taxes shall be apportioned among the several States which may be included within this Union, according to their respective Numbers, which shall be determined by adding to the whole Number of free Persons, including those bound to Service for a Term of Years, and excluding Indians not taxed, three fifths of all other Persons. (See 14th Amendment).] The actual Enumeration shall be made within three Years after the first Meeting of the Congress of the United States, and within every subsequent Term of ten Years, in such Manner as they shall by Law direct. **The Number of Representatives shall not exceed one for every thirty Thousand**, but each State shall have at Least one Representative; and until such enumeration shall be made, the State of New Hampshire shall be entitled to chuse three, Massachusetts eight, Rhode-Island and Providence Plantations one, Connecticut five, New-York six, New Jersey four, Pennsylvania eight, Delaware one, Maryland six, Virginia ten, North Carolina five, South Carolina five, and Georgia three.

[4] **When vacancies happen in the Representation from any State, the Executive Authority thereof shall** issue Writs of Election to **fill such Vacancies**.

[5] The House of Representatives shall chuse their Speaker and other Officers; and shall have the sole Power of Impeachment.

Section 3 [Senate]

[1] The Senate of the United States shall be composed of two Senators from each State, chosen by the Legislature (See 17th Amendment) thereof, for six Years; and each Senator shall have one Vote.

[2] Immediately after they shall be assembled in Consequence of the first Election, they shall be divided as equally as may be into three Classes. The Seats of the Senators of the first Class shall be vacated at the Expiration of the second Year, of the second Class at the Expiration of the fourth Year, and of the third Class

at the Expiration of the sixth Year, so that one third may be chosen every second Year; and if Vacancies happen by Resignation, or otherwise, during the Recess of the Legislature of any State, the Executive thereof may make temporary Appointments until the next Meeting of the Legislature, which shall then fill such Vacancies (See 17th Amendment).

[3] No Person shall be a Senator who shall not have attained to the Age of thirty Years, and been nine Years a Citizen of the United States, and who shall not, when elected, be an Inhabitant of that State for which he shall be chosen.

[4] The Vice President of the United States shall be President of the Senate, but shall have no Vote, unless they be equally divided.

[5] The Senate shall chuse their other Officers, and also a President pro tempore, in the Absence of the Vice President, or when he shall exercise the Office of President of the United States.

[6] The Senate shall have the sole Power to try all Impeachments. When sitting for that Purpose, they shall be on Oath or Affirmation. When the President of the United States is tried, the Chief Justice shall preside: And no Person shall be convicted without the Concurrence of two thirds of the Members present.

[7] Judgment in Cases of Impeachment shall not extend further than to removal from Office, and disqualification to hold and enjoy any Office of honor, Trust or Profit under the United States: but the Party convicted shall nevertheless be liable and subject to Indictment, Trial, Judgment and Punishment, according to Law.

Section 4 [Election of Members; Sessions]

[1] The Times, Places and Manner of holding Elections for Senators and Representatives, shall be prescribed in each State by the Legislature thereof; but the Congress may at any time by Law make or alter such Regulations, except as to the Places of chusing Senators.

[2] The Congress shall assemble at least once in every Year, and such Meeting shall be on the first Monday in December (See 20th Amendment), unless they shall by Law appoint a different Day.

Section 5 [Proceedings; Adjournment]

[1] Each House shall be the Judge of the Elections, Returns and Qualifications of its own Members, and a Majority of each shall constitute a Quorum to do Business; but a smaller Number may adjourn from day to day, and may be authorized to compel the Attendance of absent Members, in such Manner, and under such Penalties as each House may provide.

[2] Each House may determine the Rules of its Proceedings, punish its Members for disorderly Behaviour, and, with the Concurrence of two thirds, expel a Member.

[3] Each House shall keep a Journal of its Proceedings, and from time to time publish the same, excepting such Parts as may in their Judgment require Secrecy; and the Yeas and Nays of the Members of either House on any question shall, at the Desire of one fifth of those Present, be entered on the Journal.

[4] Neither House, during the Session of Congress, shall, without the Consent of the other, adjourn for more than three days, nor to any other Place than that in which the two Houses shall be sitting.

Section 6 [Congressional Compensation; Privileges; Holding other office]

[1] The Senators and Representatives shall receive a Compensation for their Services, to be ascertained by Law, and paid out of the Treasury of the United States. They shall in all Cases, except Treason, Felony and Breach of the Peace, be privileged from Arrest during their Attendance at the Session of their respective Houses, and in going to and returning from the same; and for any

Speech or Debate in either House, they shall not be questioned in any other Place.

[2] No Senator or Representative shall, during the Time for which he was elected, be appointed to any civil Office under the Authority of the United States, which shall have been created, or the Emoluments whereof shall have been encreased during such time; and no Person holding any Office under the United States, shall be a Member of either House during his Continuance in Office.

Section 7 [Bills and resolutions; Veto]

[1] All Bills for raising Revenue shall originate in the House of Representatives; but the Senate may propose or concur with Amendments as on other Bills.

[2] Every Bill which shall have passed the House of Representatives and the Senate, shall, before it become a Law, be presented to the President of the United States; If he approve he shall sign it, but if not he shall return it, with his Objections to that House in which it shall have originated, who shall enter the Objections at large on their Journal, and proceed to reconsider it. If after such Reconsideration two thirds of that House shall agree to pass the Bill, it shall be sent, together with the Objections, to the other House, by which it shall likewise be reconsidered, and if approved by two thirds of that House, it shall become a Law. But in all such Cases the Votes of both Houses shall be determined by yeas and Nays, and the Names of the Persons voting for and against the Bill shall be entered on the Journal of each House respectively. If any Bill shall not be returned by the President within ten Days (Sundays excepted) after it shall have been presented to him, the Same shall be a Law, in like Manner as if he had signed it, unless the Congress by their Adjournment prevent its Return, in which Case it shall not be a Law.

[3] Every Order, Resolution, or Vote to which the Concurrence of the Senate and House of Representatives may be necessary (except on a question of Adjournment) shall be presented to the President of the United States; and before the Same shall take Effect, shall be approved by him, or being disapproved by him, shall be repassed by two thirds of the Senate and House of Representatives, according to the Rules and Limitations prescribed in the Case of a Bill.

Section 8 [Powers of Congress]

[1] The Congress shall have Power To lay and collect Taxes, Duties, Imposts and Excises, to pay the Debts and provide for the common Defence and general Welfare of the United States; but all Duties, Imposts and Excises shall be uniform throughout the United States;

[2] To borrow Money on the credit of the United States;

[3] To regulate Commerce with foreign Nations, and among the several States, and with the Indian Tribes;

[4] To establish an uniform Rule of Naturalization, and uniform Laws on the subject of Bankruptcies throughout the United States;

[5] To coin Money, regulate the Value thereof, and of foreign Coin, and fix the Standard of Weights and Measures;

[6] To provide for the Punishment of counterfeiting the Securities and current Coin of the United States;

[7] To establish Post Offices and post Roads;

[8] To promote the Progress of Science and useful Arts, by securing for limited Times to Authors and Inventors the exclusive Right to their respective Writings and Discoveries;

[9] To constitute Tribunals inferior to the supreme Court;

[10] To define and punish Piracies and Felonies committed on the high Seas, and Offences against the Law of Nations;

[11] To declare War, grant Letters of Marque and Reprisal, and make Rules concerning Captures on Land and Water;

[12] To raise and support Armies, but no Appropriation of Money to that Use shall be for a longer Term than two Years;

[13] To provide and maintain a Navy;

[14] To make Rules for the Government and Regulation of the land and naval Forces;

[15] To provide for calling forth the Militia to execute the Laws of the Union, suppress Insurrections and repel Invasions;

[16] To provide for organizing, arming, and disciplining, the Militia, and for governing such Part of them as may be employed in the Service of the United States, reserving to the States respectively, the Appointment of the Officers, and the Authority of training the Militia according to the discipline prescribed by Congress;

[17] To exercise exclusive Legislation in all Cases whatsoever, over such District (not exceeding ten Miles square) as may, by Cession of particular States, and the Acceptance of Congress, become the Seat of the Government of the United States, and to exercise like Authority over all Places purchased by the Consent of the Legislature of the State in which the Same shall be, for the Erection of Forts, Magazines, Arsenals, dock-Yards, and other needful Buildings;--And

[18] **To make all Laws which shall be necessary and proper for carrying into Execution the foregoing Powers, and all other Powers vested by this Constitution in the Government of the United States,** or in any Department or Officer thereof.

Section 9 [Powers denied Congress]

[1] The Migration or Importation of such Persons as any of the States now existing shall think proper to admit, shall not be prohibited by the Congress prior to the Year one thousand eight hundred and eight, but a Tax or duty may be imposed on such Importation, not exceeding ten dollars for each Person.

[2] The Privilege of the Writ of Habeas Corpus shall not be suspended, unless when in Cases of Rebellion or Invasion the public Safety may require it.

[3] No Bill of Attainder or ex post facto Law shall be passed.

[4] No Capitation, or other direct, Tax shall be laid, unless in Proportion to the Census or Enumeration herein before directed to be taken (See 16th Amendment).

[5] No Tax or Duty shall be laid on Articles exported from any State.

[6] No Preference shall be given by any Regulation of Commerce or Revenue to the Ports of one State over those of another: nor shall Vessels bound to, or from, one State, be obliged to enter, clear, or pay Duties in another.

[7] No Money shall be drawn from the Treasury, but in Consequence of Appropriations made by Law; and a regular Statement and Account of the Receipts and Expenditures of all public Money shall be published from time to time.

[8] No Title of Nobility shall be granted by the United States: And no Person holding any Office of Profit or Trust under them, shall, without the Consent of the Congress, accept of any present, Emolument, Office, or Title, of any kind whatever, from any King, Prince, or foreign State.

Section 10 [Powers denied the states]

[1] No State shall enter into any Treaty, Alliance, or Confederation; grant Letters of Marque and Reprisal; coin Money; emit Bills of Credit; make any Thing but gold and silver Coin a Tender in Payment of Debts; pass any Bill of Attainder, ex post facto Law, or Law impairing the Obligation of Contracts, or grant any Title of Nobility

[2] No State shall, without the Consent of the Congress, lay any Imposts or Duties on Imports or Exports, except what may be absolutely necessary for executing its inspection Laws: and the net

Produce of all Duties and Imposts, laid by any State on Imports or Exports, shall be for the Use of the Treasury of the United States; and all such Laws shall be subject to the Revision and Controul of the Congress.

[3] No State shall, without the Consent of Congress, lay any Duty of Tonnage, keep Troops, or Ships of War in time of Peace, enter into any Agreement or Compact with another State, or with a foreign Power, or engage in War, unless actually invaded, or in such imminent Danger as will not admit of delay.

Article 2
[THE EXECUTIVE BRANCH]

Section 1. [The President]

[1] The executive Power shall be vested in a President of the United States of America. He shall hold his Office during the Term of four Years, and, together with the Vice President, chosen for the same Term, be elected, as follows:

[2] Each State shall appoint, in such Manner as the Legislature thereof may direct, a Number of Electors, equal to the whole Number of Senators and Representatives to which the State may be entitled in the Congress: but no Senator or Representative, or Person holding an Office of Trust or Profit under the United States, shall be appointed an Elector.

[3] The Electors shall meet in their respective States, and vote by Ballot for two Persons, of whom one at least shall not be an Inhabitant of the same State with Themselves. And they shall make a List of all the Persons voted for, and of the Number of Votes for each; which List they shall sign and certify, and transmit sealed to the Seat of the Government of the United States, directed to the President of the Senate. The President of the Senate shall, in the Presence of the Senate and House of Representatives, open all the Certificates, and the Votes shall them be counted.

The Person having the greatest Number of Votes shall be the President, if such Number be a Majority of the whole Number of Electors appointed; and if there be more than one who have such Majority, and have an equal Number of Votes, then the House of Representatives shall immediately chuse by Ballot one of them for President; and if no Person have a Majority, then from the five highest on the List the said House shall in like Manner chuse the President. But in chusing the President, the Votes shall be taken by States, the Representation from each State having one Vote; A quorum for this Purpose shall consist of a Member or Members from two thirds of the States, and a Majority of all the States shall be necessary to a Choice. In every Case, after the Choice of the President, the Person having the greatest Number of Votes of the Electors shall be the Vice President. But if there should remain two or more who have equal Votes, the Senate shall chuse from them by Ballot the Vice President (See 12th Amendment).

[4] The Congress may determine the Time of chusing the Electors, and the Day on which they shall give their Votes; which Day shall be the same throughout the United States.

[5] No Person except a natural born Citizen, or a Citizen of the United States, at the time of the Adoption of this Constitution, shall be eligible to the Office of President; neither shall any Person be eligible to that Office who shall not have attained to the Age of thirty five Years, and been fourteen Years a Resident within the United States.

[6] In Case of the Removal of the President from Office, or of his Death, Resignation, or Inability to discharge the Powers and Duties of the said Office, the Same shall devolve on the Vice President, and the Congress may by Law provide for the Case of Removal, Death, Resignation or Inability, both of the President and Vice President, declaring what Officer shall then act as President, and such Officer shall act accordingly, until the Disability be removed, or a President shall be elected (See 25th Amendment).

[7] The President shall, at stated Times, receive for his Services, a Compensation, which shall neither be encreased nor diminished during the Period for which he shall have been elected, and he shall not receive within that Period any other Emolument from the United States, or any of them.

[8] Before he enter on the Execution of his Office, he shall take the following Oath or Affirmation:--"I do solemnly swear (or affirm) that I will faithfully execute the Office of President of the United States, and will to the best of my Ability, preserve, protect and defend the Constitution of the United States."

Section 2. [Commander-in-Chief - Pardons -Treaties - Appointments]

[1] The President shall be Commander in Chief of the Army and Navy of the United States, and of the Militia of the several States, when called into the actual Service of the United States; he may require the Opinion, in writing, of the principal Officer in each of the executive Departments, upon any Subject relating to the Duties of their respective Offices, and he shall have Power to grant Reprieves and Pardons for Offenses against the United States, except in Cases of Impeachment.

[2] He shall have Power, by and with the Advice and Consent of the Senate, to make Treaties, provided two thirds of the Senators present concur; and he shall nominate, and by and with the Advice and Consent of the Senate, shall appoint Ambassadors, other public Ministers and Consuls, Judges of the supreme Court, and all other Officers of the United States, whose Appointments are not herein otherwise provided for, and which shall be established by Law: but the Congress may by Law vest the Appointment of such inferior Officers, as they think proper, in the President alone, in the Courts of Law, or in the Heads of Departments.

[3] The President shall have Power to fill up all Vacancies that may happen during the Recess of the Senate, by granting Commissions which shall expire at the End of their next Session.

Section 3. [Miscellaneous Powers and Duties]
He shall from time to time give to the Congress Information of the State of the Union, and recommend to their Consideration such Measures as he shall judge necessary and expedient; he may, on extraordinary Occasions, convene both Houses, or either of them, and in Case of Disagreement between them, with Respect to the Time of Adjournment, he may adjourn them to such Time as he shall think proper; he shall receive Ambassadors and other public Ministers; he shall take Care that the Laws be faithfully executed, and shall Commission all the Officers of the United States.

Section 4. [Impeachment]
The President, Vice President and all civil Officers of the United States, shall be removed from Office on Impeachment for, and Conviction of, Treason, Bribery, or other high Crimes and Misdemeanors.

Article 3
[THE JUDICIAL BRANCH]
Section 1. [Judicial Power]
The judicial Power of the United States, shall be vested in one supreme Court, and in such inferior Courts as the Congress may from time to time ordain and establish. The Judges, both of the supreme and inferior Courts, shall hold their Offices during good Behaviour, and shall, at stated Times, receive for their Services, a Compensation, which shall not be diminished during their Continuance in Office.

Section 2. [Extent; Supreme Court; Trial]

[1] The judicial Power shall extend to all Cases, in Law and Equity, arising under this Constitution, the Laws of the United States, and Treaties made, or which shall be made, under their Authority;--to all Cases affecting Ambassadors, other public Ministers and Consuls;--to all Cases of admiralty and maritime Jurisdiction; –to Controversies to which the United States shall be a Party;--to Controversies between two or more States;--between a State and

Citizens of another State (see 11ᵗʰ Amendment);--between Citizens of different States;--between Citizens of the same State claiming Lands under Grants of different States, and between a State, or the Citizens thereof, and foreign States, Citizens or Subjects.

[2] In all Cases affecting Ambassadors, other public Ministers and Consuls, and those in which a State shall be Party, the supreme Court shall have original Jurisdiction. In all the other Cases before mentioned, the supreme Court shall have appellate Jurisdiction, both as to Law and Fact, with such Exceptions, and under such Regulations as the Congress shall make.

[3] The Trial of all Crimes, except in Cases of Impeachment, shall be by Jury; and such Trial shall be held in the State where the said Crimes shall have been committed; but when not committed within any State, the Trial shall be at such Place or Places as the Congress may by Law have directed.

Section 3. [Treason; Proof and punishment]

[1] Treason against the United States, shall consist only in levying War against them, or in adhering to their Enemies, giving them Aid and Comfort. No Person shall be convicted of Treason unless on the Testimony of two Witnesses to the same overt Act, or on Confession in open Court.

[2] The Congress shall have Power to declare the Punishment of Treason, but no Attainder of Treason shall work Corruption of Blood, or Forfeiture except during the Life of the Person attainted.

Article 4
[STATE AND TERRITORIAL RELATIONS]
Section 1. [Full faith and credit]

Full Faith and Credit shall be given in each State to the public Acts, Records, and judicial Proceedings of every other State. And the Congress may by general Laws prescribe the Manner in which such Acts, Records and Proceedings shall be proved, and the Effect thereof.

Section 2. [Privileges and immunities; Fugitives]

[1] The Citizens of each State shall be entitled to all Privileges and Immunities of Citizens in the several States.

[2] A Person charged in any State with Treason, Felony, or other Crime, who shall flee from Justice, and be found in another State, shall on Demand of the executive Authority of the State from which he fled, be delivered up, to be removed to the State having Jurisdiction of the Crime.

[3] No Person held to Service or Labour in one State, under the Laws thereof, escaping into another, shall, in Consequence of any Law or Regulation therein, be discharged from such Service or Labour, but shall be delivered up on Claim of the Party to whom such Service or Labour may be due (See 13th Amendment).

Section 3. [Admission of states; Rules re: territory and states]

[1] New States may be admitted by the Congress into this Union; but no new State shall be formed or erected within the Jurisdiction of any other State; nor any State be formed by the Junction of two or more States, or Parts of States, without the Consent of the Legislatures of the States concerned as well as of the Congress.

[2] The Congress shall have Power to dispose of and make all needful Rules and Regulations respecting the Territory or other Property belonging to the United States; and nothing in this Constitution shall be so construed as to Prejudice any Claims of the United States, or of any particular State.

Section 4. [Republican form of government; Invasion and Domestic Violence] The United States shall guarantee to every State in this Union a Republican Form of Government, and shall protect each of them against Invasion; and on Application of the Legislature, or of the Executive (when the Legislature cannot be convened) against domestic Violence.

Article 5
[AMENDMENTS TO CONSTITUTION]

The Congress, whenever two thirds of both Houses shall deem it necessary, shall propose Amendments to this Constitution, or **on the Application of the Legislatures of two thirds of the several States, shall call a Convention for proposing Amendments, which**, in either Case, **shall be valid to all Intents and Purposes, as Part of this Constitution, when ratified by the Legislatures of three fourths of the several States, or by Conventions in three fourths thereof, as the one or the other Mode of Ratification may be proposed by the Congress**; Provided that no Amendment which may be made prior to the Year One thousand eight hundred and eight shall in any Manner affect the first and fourth Clauses in the Ninth Section of the first Article; and that no State, without its Consent, shall be deprived of its equal Suffrage in the Senate.

Article 6
[SUPREMACY CLAUSE; OATHS; RELIGIOUS TESTS]

All Debts contracted and Engagements entered into, before the Adoption of this Constitution, shall be as valid against the United States under this Constitution, as under the Confederation.

This Constitution, and the Laws of the United States which shall be made in Pursuance thereof; and all Treaties made, or which shall be made, under the Authority of the United States, **shall be the supreme Law of the Land**; and the Judges in every State shall be bound thereby, any Thing in the Constitution or Laws of any State to the Contrary notwithstanding.

The Senators and Representatives before mentioned, and the Members of the several State Legislatures, and all executive and judicial Officers, both of the United States and of the several States, shall be bound by Oath or Affirmation, to support this Constitution; but no religious Test shall ever be required as a Qualification to any Office or public Trust under the United States.

Article 7
[ORIGINAL RATIFICATION]

The Ratification of the Conventions of nine States, shall be sufficient for the Establishment of this Constitution between the States so ratifying the Same.

Amendment 1
[Freedom of Religion, Speech and Press; Peaceful Assembly; Petition of Grievances]

Congress shall make no law respecting an establishment of religion, or prohibiting the free exercise thereof; or abridging the freedom of speech, or of the press; or the right of the people peaceably to assemble, and to petition the Government for a redress of grievances.

Amendment 2
[Right To Bear Arms]

A well regulated Militia, being necessary to the security of a free State, the right of the people to keep and bear Arms, shall not be infringed.

Amendment 3
[Soldiers Denied Quarter in Homes]

No Soldier shall, in time of peace be quartered in any house, without the consent of the Owner, nor in time of war, but in a manner to be prescribed by law.

Amendment 4
[Search and Seizure]

The right of the people to be secure in their persons, houses, papers, and effects, against unreasonable searches and seizures, shall not be violated, and no Warrants shall issue, but upon probable cause, supported by Oath or affirmation, and particularly describing the place to be searched, and the persons or things to be seized.

Amendment 5
[Grand Jury Indictment for Capital Crimes; Double Jeopardy; Self-Incrimination; Due Process of Law; Just Compensation for Property]

No person shall be held to answer for a capital, or otherwise infamous crime, unless on a presentment or indictment of a Grand Jury, except in cases arising in the land or naval forces, or in the Militia, when in actual service in time of War or public danger; nor shall any person be subject for the same offence to be twice put in jeopardy of life or limb; nor shall be compelled in any criminal case to be a witness against himself, nor be deprived of life, liberty, or property, without due process of law; nor shall private property be taken for public use, without just compensation.

Amendment 6
[Jury trials for crimes, and procedural rights]

In all criminal prosecutions, the accused shall enjoy the right to a speedy and public trial, by an impartial jury of the State and district wherein the crime shall have been committed, which district shall have been previously ascertained by law, and to be informed of the nature and cause of the accusation; to be confronted with the witnesses against him; to have compulsory process for obtaining witnesses in his favor, and to have the Assistance of Counsel for his defence.

Amendment 7
[Civil Trials]

In Suits at common law, where the value in controversy shall exceed twenty dollars, the right of trial by jury shall be preserved, and no fact tried by a jury, shall be otherwise reexamined in any Court of the United States, than according to the rules of the common law.

Amendment 8
[Excessive Bail, Fines, Punishments]

Excessive bail shall not be required, nor excessive fines imposed, nor cruel and unusual punishments inflicted.

Amendment 9
[The People Retain Rights/No Constructive
Enlargement of Powers]

The enumeration in the Constitution, of certain rights, shall not be construed to deny or disparage others retained by the people.

Amendment 10
[Powers Reserved to States or the People]
Amendments 1-10 Passed by Congress September 25, 1789. Ratified December 15, 1791.

The powers not delegated to the United States by the Constitution, nor prohibited by it to the States, are reserved to the States respectively, or to the people.

Amendment 11
[Suits Against States]
Passed by Congress March 4, 1794. Ratified February 7, 1795.

The Judicial power of the United States shall not be construed to extend to any suit in law or equity, commenced or prosecuted against one of the United States by Citizens of another State, or by Citizens or Subjects of any Foreign State.

Amendment 12
[Presidential Electors]
Passed by Congress December 9, 1803. Ratified June 15, 1804.

The Electors shall meet in their respective states and vote by ballot for President and Vice-President, one of whom, at least, shall not be an inhabitant of the same state with themselves; they shall name in their ballots the person voted for as President, and in distinct ballots the person voted for as Vice-President, and they shall make distinct lists of all persons voted for as President, and of all persons voted for as Vice-President, and of the number of votes for each, which lists they shall sign and certify, and transmit sealed to the seat of the government of the United States, directed to the President of the Senate;--The President of the Senate shall, in the presence of the

Senate and House of Representatives, open all the certificates and the votes shall then be counted;--The person having the greatest number of votes for President, shall be the President, if such number be a majority of the whole number of Electors appointed; and if no person have such majority, then from the persons having the highest numbers not exceeding three on the list of those voted for as President, the House of Representatives shall choose immediately, by ballot, the President. But in choosing the President, the votes shall be taken by states, the representation from each state having one vote; a quorum for this purpose shall consist of a member or members from two-thirds of the states, and a majority of all the states shall be necessary to a choice. And if the House of Representatives shall not choose a President whenever the right of choice shall devolve upon them, before the fourth day of March next following, then the Vice-President shall act as President, as in the case of the death or other constitutional disability of the President (See section 3 of 20th Amendment). The person having the greatest number of votes as Vice-President, shall be the Vice-President, if such number be a majority of the whole number of Electors appointed, and if no person have a majority, then from the two highest numbers on the list, the Senate shall choose the Vice-President; a quorum for the purpose shall consist of two-thirds of the whole number of Senators, and a majority of the whole number shall be necessary to a choice. But no person constitutionally ineligible to the office of President shall be eligible to that of Vice-President of the United States.

Amendment 13
[Slavery Abolished; Enforcement]
Passed by Congress January 31, 1865. Ratified December 6, 1865.

Section 1. Neither slavery nor involuntary servitude, except as a punishment for crime whereof the party shall have been duly convicted, shall exist within the United States, or any place subject to their jurisdiction.

Section 2. Congress shall have power to enforce this article by appropriate legislation.

Amendment 14
[Citizenship; Privileges and Immunities; Due Process; Equal Protection; Apportionment of Representation; Disqualification of Officers; Public Debt; Enforcement]
Passed by Congress June 13, 1866. Ratified July 9, 1868.

Section 1. All persons born or naturalized in the United States, and subject to the jurisdiction thereof, are citizens of the United States and of the State wherein they reside. **No State shall make or enforce any law which shall abridge the privileges or immunities of citizens of the United States; nor shall any State deprive any person of life, liberty, or property, without due process of law; nor deny to any person within its jurisdiction the equal protection of the laws.**

Section 2. Representatives shall be apportioned among the several States according to their respective numbers, counting the whole number of persons in each State, excluding Indians not taxed. But when the right to vote at any election for the choice of electors for President and Vice President of the United States, Representatives in Congress, the Executive and Judicial officers of a State, or the members of the Legislature thereof, is denied to any of the male inhabitants of such State, being twenty-one years of age (See section 1 of 26th Amendment), and citizens of the United States, or in any way abridged, except for participation in rebellion, or other crime, the basis of representation therein shall be reduced in the proportion which the number of such male citizens shall bear to the whole number of male citizens twenty-one years of age in such State.

Section 3. No person shall be a Senator or Representative in Congress, or elector of President and Vice President, or hold any office, civil or military, under the United States, or under any State, who, having previously taken an oath, as a member of Congress, or as an officer of the United States, or as a member of any State legislature, or as an executive or judicial officer of any State, to support the Constitution of the United States, shall have engaged in insurrection or rebellion against the same, or given aid or comfort to the enemies thereof. But Congress may by a vote of two-thirds of each House, remove such disability.

Section 4. The validity of the public debt of the United States, authorized by law, including debts incurred for payment of pensions and bounties for services in suppressing insurrection or rebellion, shall not be questioned. But neither the United States nor any State shall assume or pay any debt or obligation incurred in aid of insurrection or rebellion against the United States, or any claim for the loss or emancipation of any slave; but all such debts, obligations and claims shall be held illegal and void.

Section 5. The Congress shall have power to enforce, by appropriate legislation, the provisions of this article.

Amendment 15
[Universal Male Suffrage]
Passed by Congress February 26, 1869. Ratified February 3, 1870.
Section 1. The right of citizens of the United States to vote shall not be denied or abridged by the United States or by any State on account of race, color, or previous condition of servitude.

Section 2. The Congress shall have power to enforce this article by appropriate legislation.

Amendment 16
[Income Tax]
Passed by Congress July 2, 1909. Ratified February 3, 1913.
The Congress shall have power to lay and collect taxes on incomes, from whatever source derived, without apportionment among the several States, and without regard to any census or enumeration.

Amendment 17
[Popular Election of Senators]
Passed by Congress May 13, 1912. Ratified April 8, 1913.

[1] The Senate of the United States shall be composed of two Senators from each State, elected by the people thereof, for six years; and each Senator shall have one vote. The electors in each State shall have the qualifications requisite for electors of the most numerous branch of the State legislatures.

[2] When vacancies happen in the representation of any State in the Senate, the executive authority of such State shall issue writs of election to fill such vacancies: *Provided*, That the legislature of any State may empower the executive thereof to make temporary appointments until the people fill the vacancies by election as the legislature may direct.

[3] This amendment shall not be so construed as to affect the election or term of any Senator chosen before it becomes valid as part of the Constitution.

Amendment 18
[Liquor Prohibition [Repealed]]
Passed by Congress December 18, 1917. Ratified January 16, 1919.
Repealed by amendment 21.

Section 1.
After one year from the ratification of this article the manufacture, sale, or transportation of intoxicating liquors within, the importation thereof into, or the exportation thereof from the United States and all territory subject to the jurisdiction thereof for beverage purposes is hereby prohibited.

Section 2.
The Congress and the several States shall have concurrent power to enforce this article by appropriate legislation.

Section 3.

This article shall be inoperative unless it shall have been ratified as an amendment to the Constitution by the legislatures of the several States, as provided in the Constitution, within seven years from the date of the submission hereof to the States by the Congress.

Amendment 19
[Women's Suffrage]
Passed by Congress June 4, 1919. Ratified August 18, 1920.

[1] The right of citizens of the United States to vote shall not be denied or abridged by the United States or by any State on account of sex.

[2] Congress shall have power to enforce this article by appropriate legislation.

Amendment 20
[Lame Duck Amendment]
Passed by Congress March 2, 1932. Ratified January 23, 1933.

Section 1. The terms of the President and Vice President shall end at noon on the 20th day of January, and the terms of Senators and Representatives at noon on the 3d day of January, of the years in which such terms would have ended if this article had not been ratified; and the terms of their successors shall then begin.

Section 2. The Congress shall assemble at least once in every year, and such meeting shall begin at noon on the 3d day of January, unless they shall by law appoint a different day.

Section 3. If, at the time fixed for the beginning of the term of the President, the President elect shall have died, the Vice President elect shall become President. If a President shall not have been chosen before the time fixed for the beginning of his term, or if the President elect shall have failed to qualify, then the Vice President elect shall act as President until a President shall have qualified; and the Congress may by law provide for the case wherein neither a President elect nor a Vice President elect shall have qualified, declaring who shall then act as President, or the manner in which one who is to act shall be selected, and such person shall act accordingly until a President or Vice President shall have qualified.

Section 4. The Congress may by law provide for the case of the death of any of the persons from whom the House of Representatives may choose a President whenever the right of choice shall have devolved upon them, and for the case of the death of any of the persons from whom the Senate may choose a Vice President whenever the right of choice shall have devolved upon them.

Section 5. Sections 1 and 2 shall take effect on the 15th day of October following the ratification of this article.

Section 6. This article shall be inoperative unless it shall have been ratified as an amendment to the Constitution by the legislatures of three-fourths of the several States within seven years from the date of its submission.

Amendment 21
[Repeal of Prohibition Amendment]
Passed by Congress February 20, 1933. Ratified December 5, 1933.
Section 1. The eighteenth article of amendment to the Constitution of the United States is hereby repealed.

Section 2. The transportation or importation into any State, Territory, or possession of the United States for delivery or use therein of intoxicating liquors, in violation of the laws thereof, is hereby prohibited.

Section 3. This article shall be inoperative unless it shall have been ratified as an amendment to the Constitution by conventions in the several

States, as provided in the Constitution, within seven years from the date of the submission hereof to the States by the Congress.

Amendment 22
[Limitation on Presidential Terms]
Passed by Congress March 21, 1947. Ratified February 27, 1951.

Section 1. No person shall be elected to the office of the President more than twice, and no person who has held the office of President, or acted as President, for more than two years of a term to which some other person was elected President shall be elected to the office of the President more than once. But this Article shall not apply to any person holding the office of President when this Article was proposed by the Congress, and shall not prevent any person who may be holding the office of President, or acting as President, during the term within which this Article becomes operative from holding the office of President or acting as President during the remainder of such term.

Section 2. This article shall be inoperative unless it shall have been ratified as an amendment to the Constitution by the legislatures of three-fourths of the several States within seven years from the date of its submission to the States by the Congress.

Amendment 23
[Presidential Electors for District of Columbia]
Passed by Congress June 16, 1960. Ratified March 29, 1961.

Section 1. The District constituting the seat of Government of the United States shall appoint in such manner as the Congress may direct:

A number of electors of President and Vice President equal to the whole number of Senators and Representatives in Congress to which the District would be entitled if it were a State, but in no event more than the least populous State; they shall be in addition to those appointed by the States, but they shall be considered, for the purposes of the election of President and Vice President, to be electors appointed by a State; and they shall meet in the District and perform such duties as provided by the twelfth article of amendment.

Section 2. The Congress shall have power to enforce this article by appropriate legislation.

Amendment 24
[Qualifications of Electors; Poll Tax]
Passed by Congress August 27, 1962. Ratified January 23, 1964.
Section 1. The right of citizens of the United States to vote in any primary or other election for President or Vice President, for electors for President or Vice President, or for Senator or Representative in Congress, shall not be denied or abridged by the United States or any State by reason of failure to pay any poll tax or other tax.

Section 2. The Congress shall have power to enforce this article by appropriate legislation.

Amendment 25
[Succession to Presidency and Vice Presidency;
Disability of President]
Passed by Congress July 6, 1965. Ratified February 10, 1967.
Section 1. In case of the removal of the President from office or of his death or resignation, the Vice President shall become President.

Section 2. Whenever there is a vacancy in the office of the Vice President, the President shall nominate a Vice President who shall take office upon confirmation by a majority vote of both Houses of Congress.

Section 3. Whenever the President transmits to the President pro tempore of the Senate and the Speaker of the House of Representatives his written declaration that he is unable to discharge the powers and duties of his office, and until he transmits to them a written declaration to the contrary, such powers and duties shall be discharged by the Vice President as Acting President.

Section 4. [1] Whenever the Vice President and a majority of either the principal officers of the executive departments or of such other body as Congress may by law provide, transmit to the President pro tempore of the Senate and the Speaker of the House of Representatives their written declaration that the President is unable to discharge the powers and duties of his office, the Vice President shall immediately assume the powers and duties of the office as Acting President.

[2] Thereafter, when the President transmits to the President pro tempore of the Senate and the Speaker of the House of Representatives his written declaration that no inability exists, he shall resume the powers and duties of his office unless the Vice President and a majority of either the principal officers of the executive department or of such other body as Congress may by law provide, transmit within four days to the President pro tempore of the Senate and the Speaker of the House of Representatives their written declaration that the President is unable to discharge the powers and duties of his office. Thereupon Congress shall decide the issue, assembling within forty-eight hours for that purpose if not in session. If the Congress, within twenty-one days after receipt of the latter written declaration, or, if Congress is not in session, within twenty-one days after Congress is required to assemble, determines by two-thirds vote of both Houses that the President is unable to discharge the powers and duties of his office, the Vice President shall continue to discharge the same as Acting President; otherwise, the President shall resume the powers and duties of his office.

Amendment 26
[Right to Vote; Citizens Eighteen Years of Age or Older]
Passed by Congress March 23, 1971. Ratified July 1, 1971.
Section 1. The right of citizens of the United States, who are eighteen years of age or older, to vote shall not be denied or abridged by the United States or by any State on account of age.

Section 2. The Congress shall have power to enforce this article by appropriate legislation.

Amendment 27
[Compensation of Senators and Representatives]
Originally proposed Sept. 25, 1789. Ratified May 7, 1992.
No law, varying the compensation for the services of the Senators and Representatives, shall take effect, until an election of Representatives shall have intervened.

ENDNOTES

INTRODUCTION

1. 2 Max Farrand (ed.), *The Records of the Federal Convention of 1787*, at p. 69, Yale University Press, New Haven, Connecticut (1911).

2. See U.S. Const., Tenth Amendment.

3. Donald S. Lutz, *Popular Consent and Popular Control*, at p. 6, Louisiana State University Press, Baton Rouge, Louisiana (1980).

4. I use the term "check and balance system" to describe the U.S. Constitution's system of checks and balances.

5. The Federalist No. 51, at p. 316 (J. Madison) (G. Wills ed. 1982).

6. James Madison uses the term "representative republic" prominently in The Federalist No. 48 to describe our intended system of free government. The Federalist No. 48, at pp. 300-302 (J. Madison) (G. Wills ed. 1982).

7. The Federalist No. 57, at p. 347 (J. Madison) (G. Wills ed. 1982).

8. The Federalist No. 26, at pp. 153-154: "Is it probable that it would be persevered in, and transmitted along through all the successive variations in a representative body, which biennial elections would naturally produce in both houses?" (A. Hamilton) (G. Wills ed. 1982).

9. The Federalist No. 52, at p. 320 (J. Madison) (G. Wills ed. 1982).

10. *The Federalist Papers*, at pp xvi-xx (A. Hamilton, J. Madison, J. Jay), Bantam Dell, New York, N.Y. (G. Wills ed. 1982).

11. Glendon, Gordon & Osakwe, *Comparative Legal Traditions*, at p. 726, West Publishing Co., St. Paul, Minn. (1985).

12. George Washington's Farewell Address, Senate Document No. 106–21, at pp. 18-19, Washington, D.C. (2000) (emphasis added.)

13. Lutz, supra, at pp. 5-6, 14.

14. Id., at p. 6.

15. Id., at pp. 8-12, 14.

16. The Federalist No. 10, at pp. 52-57 (J. Madison) (G. Wills ed. 1982).

17. The Federalist No. 57, at p. 347 (J. Madison) (G. Wills ed. 1982).

18. See, for example, George Washington's Farewell Address, supra, at p. 15; The Federalist No. 70, at p. 426 (A. Hamilton) (Wells, ed.)

19. Helen E. Veit; Kenneth R. Bowling; Charlene Bangs Bickford (eds.), *Creating The Bill of Rights: The Documentary Record from the First Federal Congress*, at pp. 77-78, The Johns Hopkins University Press, Baltimore, Maryland (1991) (emphasis added).

20. The Federalist No. 49, at pp. 306-307 (J. Madison) (G. Wills ed. 1982).

21. Gordon S. Wood, *The Creation of the American Republic 1776-1789*, at pp. 4-7, The University of North Carolina Press, Chapel Hill, North Carolina (1969).

22. U.S. Const., Article VI.

CHAPTER I

1. 2 Max Farrand (ed.), *The Records of the Federal Convention of 1787*, at p. 632, Yale University Press, New Haven, Connecticut (1911).

2. U.S. Constitution, Article V.

3. Helen E. Veit; Kenneth R. Bowling; Charlene Bangs Bickford (eds.), *Creating The Bill of Rights*, at pp. 5, 11-14 69-86, The Johns Hopkins University Press, Baltimore, Maryland (1991).

4. *Id.*, at pp. 6-11.

5. *Id.*, at pp. ix, xi.

6. *Id.*, at p. ix.

7. Richard P. Bernstein, *The Sleeper Wakes: The History and Legacy of the Twenty-Seventh Amendment*, at pp. 515-531, 61 Fordham L. Rev. 497 (1992).

8. Veit, supra, at pp. 233-234 (emphasis added); see also http://www.archives.gov/exhibits/american_originals/inaugtxt.html

9. 1 Max Farrand (ed.), *The Records of the Federal Convention of 1787*, at pp. 1-17, Yale University Press, New Haven, Connecticut (1911).

10. The Federalist Nos. 39, 55, 56, and 58 (J. Madison); The Federalist No. 84 (A. Hamilton); see U.S. Const., at Article IV, section 4.

11. The Federalist No. 39, at p.228 (J. Madison) (G. Wills ed. 1982).

Chapter 2

1. The Federalist No. 43, at p. 268 (J. Madison) (G. Wills ed. 1982) (emphasis added.)

2. Helen E. Veit; Kenneth R. Bowling; Charlene Bangs Bickford (eds.), *Creating The Bill of Rights*, The Johns Hopkins University Press, Baltimore, Maryland (1991), at pp. 3-4, 11, 49-50; see also http://www.archives.gov/exhibits/charters/bill_of_rights.htmlhttp://www.archives.gov/exhibits/charters/bill_of_rights.html;.

3. http://www.archives.gov/exhibits/charters/constitution_q_and_a.html; U.S. Const., Article VII.

4. 2 Max Farrand (ed.), *The Records of the Federal Convention of 1787*, Yale University Press, New Haven, Connecticut (1911), at pp. 479, 561, 564, 631, 634.

5. Veit, supra, at pp. xi-xii.

6. *Id.*, at pp. xii-xvi; Richard P. Bernstein, *The Sleeper Wakes: The History and Legacy of the Twenty-Seventh Amendment*, 61 Fordham L. Rev. 497, 513-525 (1992).

7. Veit, supra, at p. 11.

8. http://www.usconstitution.net/constamrat.html

9. U.S.C.A. Const., Vol. 1, at p. 29; see also http://www.archives.gov/exhibits/charters/bill_of_rights.htmlhttp://www.archives.gov/exhibits/charters/bill_of_rights.html;.

10. Richard L. Burke, The Los Angeles Times, *1789 Amendment is Ratified But Now the Debate Begins*, May 8, 1992; Bernstein, supra, at p. 498.

11. Los Angeles Times, *Los Angeles Riots: 20 Years Later,* April 28, 2014, http://www.latimes.com/la-me-los-angeles-riots-sg-storygallery. html; see also http://www.southcentralhistory.com/la-riots.php.

12. Bernstein, supra, at p. 499, fn. 6.

13. U.S. Constitution, Amendment 27.

14. Amend. I U.S.C.A., Historical Notes to Article I, at p. 38; Bernstein, supra, at p. 532; http://www.archives.gov/exhibits/charters/bill_of_ rights.html.

15. U.S. Constitution, Article V.

16. Bernstein, supra, at p. 534.

17. *Ibid.*

19. Bernstein, supra, at pp. 534-535.

20. *Id.,* at pp. 536-537.

21. *Ibid.*

22. *Id.,* at p. 537.

23. *Id.,* at pp. 536-539, 542.

24. *Id.,* at p. 537.

25. *Ibid.*

26. *Ibid.*

27. *Id.*, at p. 538.

28. *Id.*, at p. 539.

29. Veit, supra, at p. 6.

30. *Ibid.*; *Id.*, at pp. 29-33.

31. *Id.*, at pp. 7-8.

32. *Id.*, at pp. 8-9, 37.

33. *Id.*, at p. 37.

34. *Id.*, at pp. 10, 45-49.

35. *Id.*, at p. 48.

36. *Id.*, at pp. 9, 37.

37. *Id.*, at pp. 10, 46, 48.

38. *Id.*, at pp. 3, 11.

40. U. S. Const., Article IV, Section 4.

41. The Federalist No. 10, at p. 56, (J. Madison) (G. Wills ed. 1982) (emphasis added.) See also The Federalist No. 48, at p. 302, (J. Madison) (G. Wills ed. 1982): "But **in a representative republic**, where the executive magistracy is carefully limited, both in the extent and the duration of its power; and **where the legislative power is exercised by an assembly** which is inspired by a supposed influence over the people, with an intrepid confidence in its own strength; **which is sufficiently**

numerous to feel all the passions which actuate a multitude; yet not so numerous as to be incapable of pursuing the objects of its passions, by means which reason prescribes; it is against the enterprising ambition of this department, that the people ought to indulge all their jealousy, and exhaust all their precautions." (emphasis added.)

42. U.S. Const., Article I, Section 2, paragraph 3.

43. The Federalist No. 55, at pp. 337-340, (J. Madison) (G. Wills ed. 1982) (emphasis added.)

44. The Federalist No. 85, at p. 537, (A. Hamilton) (G. Wills ed. 1982).

45. The Federalist No. 56, at pp. 342, 343, 345, 347, respectively by each part of quote (J. Madison) (G. Wills ed. 1982) (emphasis added.)

46. The Federalist No. 58, at 354 (J. Madison) (G. Wills ed. 1982) (emphasis added.)

47. U.S. Const., Article IV, Section 4.

48. 2 Farrand, supra, at pp. 637, fn. 21, 638.

49. 1 Max Farrand (ed.), *The Records of the Federal Convention of 1787*, Yale University Press, New Haven, Connecticut (1911), at pp. 2-3, 5.

50. 2 Farrand, supra, at p. 644, footnote, which reads: "This was the only occasion on which the President entered at all into the discussions of the convention."

51. *Id.*, at pp. 643-644.

52. *Id.*, at p. 644.

53. *Ibid.*

54. *Ibid.*

CHAPTER 3

1. 2 M. Farrand (ed.), *The Records of the Federal Convention of 1787*, at pp. 629-631.

2. In an August 23, 1823 letter from James Madison to George Hay, Madison acknowledges that the Framers "in the latter stage of the Session," experienced "a degree of the hurrying influence produced by fatigue and impatience in all such Bodies . . ." http://www.loc.gov/resource/mjm.20_0530_0532.

3. 2 M. Farrand, supra, at pp. 177, 565.

4. *Id.*, at p. 590, fn. 8.

5. *Id.*, at p. 590.

6. 3 *Debates on The Adoption of the Federal Constitution* at pp. 1, 21-22, (J. Elliot ed. 1888) [hereinafter "ELLIOT'S DEBATES"].

7. Id., at p. 94 (emphasis added.)

8. The Federalist No. 49, at p. 306 (J. Madison) (G. Wills ed. 1982).

9. George Washington's Farewell Address, Senate Document No. 106–21, at p. 13, Washington, D.C. (2000) (emphasis added.)

10. The Ninth Amendment uses language of "rights," while the Tenth Amendment uses language of "powers." The original meaning of

the Ninth Amendment, however, was understood to limit govern-ment by prohibiting the constructive enlargement of federal power. See, for example, Kurt T. Lash, *The Lost Original Meaning of the Ninth Amendment*, 83 Texas L. Rev. 331 (December 2004).

11. 1 M. Farrand (ed.), *The Records of the Federal Convention of 1787*, at pp. 202-203.

12. The Federalist Number 43, at p. 268 (J. Madison) (G. Wills ed. 1982).

13. George Washington's Inaugural Address, April 30, 1789, at para. 5, Helen E. Veit; Kenneth R. Bowling; Charlene Bangs Bickford (eds.), *Creating The Bill of Rights*, at pp. 233-234, The Johns Hopkins University Press, Baltimore, Maryland (1991); http://www.archives. gov/exhibits/american_originals/inaugtxt.html; The Federalist Nos. 37, 43 and 85.

14. 2 M. Farrand (ed.), *The Records of the Federal Convention of 1787*, at pp. 547, 553-554, 578, 581-582, 585, 602; 1 M. Farrand (ed.), *The Records of the Federal Convention of 1787*, at p. xxiii.

15. *Id.*, at pp. 629-631, 633 fn. 16, 634.

16. Michael Stokes Paulsen, *A General Theory of Article V: The Constitutional Lessons of the Twenty-Seventh Amendment*, 103 Yale L. J. 677, 761 (1993).

17. 1 M. Farrand, supra, at pp. 20-22.

18. *Id.*, at p. 20.

19. 19.18. *Id.*, at p. 22.

20. *Id.*, at pp. 121-122.

21. *Id.*, at pp. 202-203. The abbreviated phrase "nem. con." means without objection.

22. *Id.*, at pp. 235-237.

23. *Id.*, at p. xxii.

24. *Ibid.*; 2 M. Farrand, supra, at pp. 97, 106, 117-118, 128.

25. 2 M. Farrand, supra, at pp. 117-118, 128, 175-177.

26. *Id.*, at pp. 129-175.

27. *Id.*, at p. 148.

28. *Id.*, at pp. 159, 174.

29. *Id.*, at p. 188.

30. *Id.*, at pp. 643, 647-649.

31. *Id.*, at pp. 467-468.

32. *Id.*, at pp. 547, 553-554.

33. *Id.*, at pp. 582, 585, 590-603.

34. *Id.*, at pp. 557-558.

35. *Id.*, at p. 558.

36. *Ibid.*

37. *Ibid.*, at pp. 558-559.

38. *Ibid.*, at p. 559.

39. *Id.*, at p. 559.

40. *Id.*, at p. 415, fn. 8; 3 M. Farrand, supra, at pp. 160-161, 210-212, 377-379, 436-437.

41. 2 M. Farrand, supra at pp. 571-572, 656-657.

42. The author counts five slave clauses in the U.S. Constitution: 1) The Three-Fifths Clause at Article I, Section 2, paragraph 3; 2) The Escaped Slave Clause at Article IV, Section 2, paragraph 3; 3) The twenty year guarantee in Article V of no changes to the first and fourth clauses in Article I, Section 9; 4) The Slave Importation Clause in Article I, Section 9, paragraph 1; and 5) Article I, Section 9, paragraph 4, which requires direct taxes to be based on the Census counting slaves as three-fifths of a person, which protected the slave states from being taxed at one-hundred percent of the "slave count."

43. 2 M. Farrand, supra, at p. 578.

44. *Ibid.*, at p. 602.

45. *Ibid.*, at p. 650; 3 Max Farrand (ed.), *The Records of the Federal Convention of 1787*, at p. 81, Yale University Press, New Haven, Connecticut (1911).

46. http://teachingamericanhistory.org/convention/citytavern/

47. 2 M. Farrand, supra, at p. 633, fn. 16.

48. 1 M. Farrand, supra, at p. 2, fn.1.

49. 2 M. Farrand, supra, at p. 328.

50. *Ibid.*

51. *Id.*, at p. 406.

52. *Id.*, at pp. 629-631(some abbreviations in original text spelled out for clarity.)

53. *Id.*, at p. 630.

54. *Id.*, at p. 631.

55. *Id.*, at pp. 631-640.

56. Thomas H. Neale, *The Article V Convention to Propose Constitutional Amendments: Contemporary Issues for Congress*, at p. 32, Congressional Research Service, July 9, 2012; Thomas H. Neale, *The Article V Convention for Proposing Constitutional Amendments: Historical Perspectives for Congress*, at p. 21, Congressional Research Service, October 22, 2012.

57. *"Congressional Research Belongs to the Public,"* The New York Times (June 17, 2015), http://nyti.ms/1MKeJp6.

CHAPTER 4
1. 1 M. Farrand (ed.), *The Records of the Federal Convention of 1787*, at p. 202-203, Yale University Press, New Haven, Connecticut (1911); 2 M.

Farrand (ed.), *The Records of the Federal Convention of 1787*, at p. 629, Yale University Press, New Haven, Connecticut (1911).

2. Bruce M. Van Sickle; Lynn M. Boughey, *A Lawful and Peaceful Revolution: Article V and Congress' Present Duty to Call a Convention For Proposing Amendments*, 14 Hamline L. Rev. 1, at pp. 25-26 (1990).

3. U.S. Const., Article I, Section 2, paragraph 3, as modified by U.S. Const., 14th Amendment, Section 2.

4. The Federalist No. 58, at pp. 353-354, (J. Madison) (G. Wills ed. 1982) (emphasis added.)

5. The Federalist No. 10, at p. 56 (J. Madison) (G. Wills ed. 1982)

6. 1 M. Farrand (ed.), supra, at pp. 20-22.

7. *Id.*, at pp. 1-4, 7-13, 15-17.

8. U.S. Constitution, Preamble, 9th and 10th Amendments.

9. James Kenneth Rogers, *The Other Way to Amend the Constitution: The Article V Constitutional Convention Amendment Process*, 30 Harvard J. of L. & P. P. 1005, 1022 (2007); see also ABA Special Constitutional Convention Study Committee, *Amendment of the Constitution by the Convention Method under Article V* (1974).

10. *Reynolds v. Sims*, 377 U.S. 533 (1964); *Lucas v. Forty-Fourth General Assembly*, 377 U.S. 713 (1964).

11. Rogers, supra, at p. 1009; Note, *Proposed Legislation on the Convention Method of Amending the United States Constitution*, 85 Harvard L. R. 1612 (1972).

12. Rogers, supra, at p. 1009; Thomas H. Neale, *The Article V Convention for Proposing Constitutional Amendments: Historical Perspectives for Congress*, at pp. 10-12, Congressional Research Service, October 22, 2012.

13. *Ibid.*

14. *Ibid.*

15. Rogers, supra, at p. 1010; Neale, supra, at pp. 12-14.

16. *Ibid.*

17. *Ibid.*; Michael Stokes Paulsen, *How to Count to Thirty-Four: The Constitutional Case for a Constitutional Convention*, 34 Harvard Journal of Law & Public Policy 837, 856 (2011).

18. S. 2307, 90th Congress (1967), which can be found at 68 Michigan L. Rev. 875, 896-902; S. 623, 91st Cong., 1st Sess. (1969); S. 215, 92nd Cong., 1st Sess. (1971); S. 1272, 93rd Cong., 1st Sess. (1973); S. 1815, 94th Cong., 1st Sess. (1975); S. 1880, 95th Cong., 1st Sess. (1977); S. 1710, 96th Cong., 1st Sess. (1979) (Hatch); S. 600, 97th Cong., 1st Sess. (1981); S. 817, 97th Cong., 1st Sess., (1981) (Hatch); H.R. 353, 97th Cong., 1st Sess., (1981); S. 119, 98th Cong., 1st Sess., (1983); S. 2812, 98th Cong., 1st Sess. (1984); S. 40, 99th Cong., 1st Sess. (1985); H.R. 351, 99th Cong., 1st Sess. (1985); S. 589, 100th Cong., 1st Sess. (1987); S. 204, 101st Cong., 1st Sess. (1989); S. 214, 102nd Cong., 1st Sess. (1991).

19. S. 2307, 90th Congress (1967).

20. The Federalist No. 43, at p. 268 (J. Madison) (G. Wills ed. 1982).

21. Pew Research Center, November, 2015, *"Beyond Distrust: How Americans View Their Government,"* at p. 72.

22. *"75% in U.S. See Widespread Government Corruption,"* Gallup (September 19, 2015), http://www.gallup.com/poll/185759/widespread-government-corruption.aspx.

23. Frank Newport, *"Half in U.S. Continue to Say Government is an Immediate Threat,"* Gallup (September 21, 2015), http://www.gallup.com/poll/185720/half-continue-say-gov-immediate-threat.aspx.

24. Jeffrey M. Jones, *"Trust in Federal Government on Domestic Matters Edges to New Low,"* Gallup (September 24, 2015), http://www.gallup.com/poll/185876/trust-federal-gov-domestic-matters-edges-new-low.aspx.

25. Jim Norman, *"Public Remains Wary of Federal Government's Power,"* Gallup (October 9, 2015), http://www.gallup.com/poll/186065/public-remains-wary-federal-government-power.aspx.

26. Justin McCarthy, *"No Improvement in Congress Approval, at 13%,"* Gallup (March 9, 2016), http://www.gallup.com/poll/189848/no-improvement-congress-approval.aspx.

27. Jeffrey M. Jones, *"Democratic, Republican Identification Near Historical Lows,"* Gallup (January 11, 2016), http://www.gallup.com/poll/188096/democratic-republican-identification-near-historical-lows.aspx.

28. Sabrina Tavarnise, *"Disparity in Life Spans of the Rich and the Poor is Growing,"* The New York Times (February 12, 2016), http://nyti.ms/1RwgE6h.

29. *Ibid.*

30. Ben Casselman, *"The Slow Death of American Entrepreneurship,"* FiveThirtyEight (May 15, 2014), http://fivethirtyeight.com/features/the-slow-death-of-american-entrepreneurship/.

31. Pew Research Center, November, 2015, *"Beyond Distrust: How Americans View Their Government,"* at pp. 72, 80-81.

32. *Citizen's United v. Federal Election Commission*, 580 U.S. 310 (2010).

33. Restatement (Second) of Contracts, §§ 151 - 153, 155 (1981).

34. *Id.*, at § 155.

35. Restatement (Second) of Contracts, § 76, Comment b (1981).

36. Glendon, Gordon & Osakwe, *Comparative Legal Traditions*, at pp. 726-727, West Publishing Co., St. Paul, Minn. (1985); Glendon, Gordon & Osakwe, *Comparative Legal Traditions in a Nutshell*, at pp. 273, 367-368, West Publishing Co., St. Paul, Minn. (1982).

37. Lectures with Professor Christopher Osakwe, "Socialist Law," University of San Diego International and Comparative Law Institute, Russia-Poland Program, Summer 1990.

38. Glendon, Gordon & Osakwe, *Comparative Legal Traditions in a Nutshell*, supra, at pp. 294.

CHAPTER 5

1. The Federalist No. 51, at p. 316 (J. Madison) (G. Wills ed. 1982) (emphasis added.)

2. 2 Max Farrand (ed.), *The Records of the Federal Convention of 1787*, at pp. 643-644, Yale University Press, New Haven, Connecticut (1911).

3. The Federalist No. 10, at p. 56 (J. Madison) (G. Wills ed. 1982).

4. 3 Max Farrand (ed.), *The Records of the Federal Convention of 1787*, at p. 586, fn. 2, Yale University Press, New Haven, Connecticut (1911); Max Farrand, *The Framing of the Constitution of the United States*, at p. 61, Yale University Press, New Haven, Connecticut (1913).

6. The Federalist No. 84, at p. 529 (A. Hamilton) (G. Wills ed. 1982) (emphasis added).

7. The Federalist No. 51, at p. 316 (J. Madison) (G. Wills ed. 1982) (emphasis added).

8. Some scholars may quibble that the use of the term "tricameralism" is improper because in a true tricameral legislative system, the third division of the legislature would actually have the ability to vote upon and approve legislation. Here, I use the term in a more generic sense. In this version of a tricameral system, the third division would not actually vote on proposed legislation in the traditional sense of the term, but would have check and balance powers designed to recompetivize the political system and reestablish the foundations of our check and balance system.

9. See U.S. Const., Article I, Section 2, paragraph 3.

10. The Federalist No. 85, at pp. 536-537 (A. Hamilton) (G. Wills ed. 1982).

11. Helen E. Veit; Kenneth R. Bowling; Charlene Bangs Bickford (eds.), *Creating The Bill of Rights*, at pp. 233-234, The Johns Hopkins

University Press, Baltimore, Maryland (1991); http://www.archives. gov/exhibits/american_originals/inaugtxt.html.

Chapter 6

1. 2 Max Farrand (ed.), *The Records of the Federal Convention of 1787*, at p. 644, Yale University Press, New Haven, Connecticut (1911).

2. For a more detailed background of this section and the history of President Roosevelt and his "court packing" plan, see David M. Kennedy, *Freedom From Fear: The American People in Depression and War, 1929-1945*, at pp. 323-337, Oxford University Press, New York, N.Y. (1999).

3. Kennedy, supra, at p. 329; *Morehead v. New York ex rel. Tipaldo*, 298 U.S. 587 (1936).

4. Kennedy, supra, at p. 334; *West Coast Hotel v. Parrish*, 300 U.S. 379 (1937).

5. *Id.*, at p. 335 (emphasis added.)

6. *Id.*, at pp. 335-337.

7. *Wickard v. Filburn*, 317 U.S. 111 (1942).

8. David S. Law, Mila Versteeg, *The Declining Influence of the United States Constitution*, 87 New York Univ. L. Rev. 762, 805 (2012).

9. Akhil Reed Amar, *The Bill of Rights as a Constitution*, 100 Yale L. J. 1131, 1162-1173 (1991).

10. *District of Columbia v. Heller*, 554 U.S. 570 (2008).

11. U.S. Const., Second Amendment.

12. *District of Columbia v. Heller*, supra, at p. 635.

13. *Id.*, at p. 595.

14. *Id.*, at p. 637.

15. *Id.*, at p. 640.

16. U.S. Const., Article I, Section 6, paragraph 1.

17. U.S. Const., Article I, Section 2, paragraph 3.

18. *Citizens United v. Federal Election Commission*, 558 U.S. 310 (2010).

19. *Id.*, at p. 360.

20. See Chapter 4, endnotes 21-31.

21. *Americans' Views on Money in Politics*, New York Times (June 2, 2015), http://nyti.ms/1KAz5AE.

22. See George Washington's Farewell Address, Senate Document No. 106–21, Washington, D.C. (2000), pp. 16-19.

23. *Id.*, at pp. 16-17.

24. *Id.*, at pp. 18-19 (emphasis added.)

25. Jeffrey M. Jones, *Democratic, Republican Identification Near Historical Lows*, Gallup, January 11, 2016, http://www.gallup.com/poll/188096/democratic-republican-identification-near-historical-lows.aspx.

26. *Korematsu v. United States*, 323 U.S. 214 (1944).

Chapter 7

1. George Washington's Farewell Address, Senate Document No. 106–21, Washington, D.C. (2000), p. 13.

2. 3 Max Farrand (ed.), *The Records of the Federal Convention of 1787*, at pp. 586-590, 586 at fn. 2, Yale University Press, New Haven, Connecticut (1911).

3. 1 Max Farrand (ed.), *The Records of the Federal Convention of 1787*, at p. xi, Yale University Press, New Haven, Connecticut (1911).

4. U.S. Const., Article I, Section 2, paragraph 1.

5. Donald S. Lutz, *Popular Consent and Popular Control*, Louisiana State University Press, Baton Rouge, Louisiana (1980), at p. 90-91.

6. *Ibid.*

7. *Id.*, at p. 91.

8. *Ibid*

9. Id., at p. 103, fn. 15, which indicates a multiple of 50 to translate one pound in 1775 to an American dollar in 1965; United States Department of Labor, Bureau of Labor Statistics, CPI Inflation Calculator, at http://www.bls.gov/data/inflation_calculator.htm, which sets forth a multiple of just over 7.5 to calculate a 1965 dollar into a 2015 dollar. Dollar equivalents stated in this chapter are approximate based on these guidelines.

6. Lutz, *Popular Consent and Popular Control*, supra at p. 101.

7. *Id.*, at pp. 102-103, 103 at fn. 14 (emphasis added.)

8. *Id.*, at p. 90.

9. Everett McKinley Dirksen, *The Supreme Court and The People*, 66 Michigan L. Rev. 837, 838 (1968).

CHAPTER 8

1. 3 Max Farrand (ed.), *The Records of the Federal Convention of 1787*, at p. 127, Yale University Press, New Haven, Connecticut (1911).

2. U.S. Const., Article V.

3. See, for example, *Reynolds v. Sims*, 377 U.S. 533 (1964); *Lucas v. Forty-Fourth General Assembly*, 377 U.S. 713 (1964)); *Wesberry v. Sanders*, 276 U.S. 1 (1964); *Gray v. Sanders*, 372 U.S. 368 (1963).

4. David S. Law, Mila Versteeg, *The Declining Influence of the United States Constitution*, 87 New York Univ. L. Rev. 762, 807 (2012), quoting Sanford Levinson, *Our Undemocratic Constitution* 21 (2006).

5. The Federalist No. 43, at p. 268 (J. Madison) (G. Wills ed. 1982).

6. 2 Max Farrand (ed.), *The Records of the Federal Convention of 1787*, at pp. 558-559, Yale University Press, New Haven, Connecticut (1911).

7. The Federalist No. 43, at p. 268 (J. Madison) (G. Wills ed. 1982).

8. For example, a simple amendment proposed by Congress, along these lines: "Any Article V convention operating as of December 31, 20xx, shall cease operations and a new vote by the state legislatures pursuant to Article V for a convention must take place before a new Article V convention begins," and ratified by three-quarters of the state legislatures would be enough to constitutionally end any open Article V convention.

9. Akhil Reed Amar, *The Bill of Rights as a Constitution*, 100 Yale L. J. 1131, 1145-1146 (1991); Richard P. Bernstein, *The Sleeper Wakes: The History and Legacy of the Twenty-Seventh Amendment*, 61 Fordham L. Rev. 497, 530 (1992).

CHAPTER 9

1. 2 Max Farrand (ed.), *The Records of the Federal Convention of 1787*, at p. 558, Yale University Press, New Haven, Connecticut (1911).

2. *Id.*, at p. 630.

3. *M'Culloch v. Maryland*, 17 U.S. 316, 402-405, 428-432 (1819); *U.S. Term Limits, Inc. v. Thornton*, 514 U.S. 779, 794-795, 820-822, 836-845 (1995).

4. The Federalist No. 59, at p. 360 (A. Hamilton) (G. Wills ed. 1982).

5. Kurt T. Lash, *The Lost Original Meaning of the Ninth Amendment*, 83 Texas L. Rev. 331, 370 (December 2004) (emphasis added.)

6. *Reynolds v. Sims*, 377 U.S. 533 (1964); *Lucas v. Forty-Fourth General Assembly*, 377 U.S. 713 (1964).

7. See Appendix 2, August 6, September 10 and September 15, 1787; 2 Max Farrand, supra, at pp. 188, 555-559, 629-631.

8. 2 Farrand, supra, at p. 559 (emphasis added.)

9. *Id.*, at p. 629.

10. *Ibid.*

11. *Id.*, at p. 630.

12. *Ibid.*

13. *Id.*, at p. 557-558.

14. Gordon S. Wood, *The Creation of the American Republic 1776-1789*, at pp. 306-389, 532-536, The University of North Carolina Press, Chapel Hill, North Carolina (1969); *M'Culloch v. Maryland*, supra, at 17 U.S. 403.

15. 1 Max Farrand (ed.), *The Records of the Federal Convention of 1787*, at p. 22, Yale University Press, New Haven, Connecticut (1911) (emphasis added.)

16. *Id.*, at p. 202.

17. 2 Farrand, supra, at p. 629.

18. U.S. Const., Article V. Here, the Call of the plenary Convention by Congress is not counted as a stage, because the Call is considered a ministerial duty to count and announce.

19. Lawrence H. Tribe, *American Constitutional Law*, at p. 298, The Foundation Press, Inc., Mineola, New York (1988).

20. Helen E. Veit; Kenneth R. Bowling; Charlene Bangs Bickford (eds.), *Creating The Bill of Rights*, at pp. 14, 15, 16, 19 and 21-22, The Johns Hopkins University Press, Baltimore, Maryland (1991).

21. Arthur Earl Bonfield, *The Dirksen Amendment and the Article V Convention Process*, 66 Michigan L. Rev. 949, 950 (1968); Charles L. Black, Jr., *Amending The Constitution: A Letter to a Congressman*, 82 Yale L. J. 189 (1972); Walter E. Dellinger, *The Recurring Question of the "Limited" Constitutional Convention*, 88 Yale L. J. 1623 (1979); Bruce

M. Van Sickle; Lynn M. Boughey, *A Lawful and Peaceful Revolution: Article V and Congress' Present Duty to Call a Convention For Proposing Amendments*, 14 Hamline L. Rev. 1 (1990); Michael Stokes Paulsen, *A General Theory of Article V: The Constitutional Lessons of the Twenthy-Seventh Amendment*, 103 Yale L. J. 677 (1993); James Kenneth Rogers, *The Other Way to Amend the Constitution: The Article V Constitutional Convention Amendment Process*, 30 Harvard J. of L. & P. P. 1005 (2007). There is dispute among lawyers and professors on the extent to which the U.S. Congress or the state legislatures may limit an Article V convention. It is the existence of the dispute itself which should cause the legal profession to act to lead the American People to an appropriate remedy. From the perspective of a working government which protects liberties, formulating a clear rule is what encourages humans to follow the rule of law.

22. Everett McKinley Dirksen, *The Supreme Court and The People*, 66 Michigan L. Rev. 837, 867 (1968); Sam J. Ervin, Jr., *Proposed Legislation to Implement the Convention Method of Amending the Constitution*, 66 Michigan L. Rev. 875, 879 (1968); Paul G. Kauper, *The Alternative Amendment Process: Some Observations*, 66 Michigan L. Rev. 903 (1968).

23. The Federalist No. 85, at p. 537 (A. Hamilton) (G. Wills ed. 1982) (emphasis added.)

24. *United States v. Sprague*, 282 U.S. 716 (1931).

25. *Id.*, at p. 730 (emphasis added.)

26. 2 Farrand, supra, at pp. 629-630.

27. 3 *Debates on The Adoption of the Federal Constitution*, at p. 94, Washington, D.C. (J. Elliot ed. 1836) ["ELLIOT'S DEBATES"] (emphasis added.) Madison confirmed these views in the Federalist No. 46 [". . . the

ultimate authority . . . resides in the people alone . . ."] and the Federalist No. 49 [" . . . the people are the only legitimate fountain of power . . ."].

28. U.S. Const., Article I, Section 8, paragraph 18 (emphasis added.)

29. The Harvard Law Review said it succinctly: "[A]ny requirement imposed by Congress which is not necessary for Congress to bring a convention into existence or to choose the mode of ratification is outside Congress' constitutional authority." Note, *Proposed Legislation on the Convention Method of Amending the United States Constitution*, 85 Harvard L. R. 1612, 1633 (1972). [This author does not approve of that line of scholarly publications which assume states and Congress may together limit the subject matter of Article V conventions based on a theory of "reasonable inference." See, Eg:, Note, *Proposed Legislation on the Convention Method of Amending the United States Constitution*, 85 Harvard L. R. 1612, 1617 (1972).]

30. *District of Columbia v. Heller*, 554 U.S. 570 (2008).

31. Lash , supra, at p. 336, citing to James Madison, *Writings*, at p. 489 (Jack N. Rakove ed., 1999).

32. U.S. Const., Article I, Section 8, paragraph 18.

33. Lash, supra, at p. 356.

34. There is a tension between the possible expansion of power through the Necessary and Proper Clause, and the limit on expansive inter-pretation of power of the Ninth Amendment. The barrier between the two is not well-defined. Apparently, instead of going back and continuing to work the problem, our so called representatives have decided for the rest of us that we are going to allow 5 of 9 Supreme

Court Justices utilize their personal biases to determine these contours and definitions.

Note also the mirror image of stating the Ninth Amendment in terms of rights and stating it in terms of powers. Because powers work upon rights, "no reduction of rights" basically means the same thing as "no enlargement of powers." See Lash, *supra*, at pp. 333, fn. 7, 337.

35. Akhil Reed Amar, *The Bill of Rights as a Constitution*, 100 Yale L. J. 1131, 1200 (1991).

36. George Washington's Farewell Address, Senate Document No. 106–21, Washington, D.C. (2000), p. 13.

37. http://www.archives.gov/exhibits/american_originals/inaugtxt.html, at p. 2.

38. Michael Stokes Paulsen, *A General Theory of Article V: The Constitutional Lessons of the Twenty-Seventh Amendment*, 103 Yale L. J. 677, 739 (1993) citing William W. Van Alstyne, *Does Article V Restrict the States to Calling Unlimited Conventions Only? – A Letter to a Colleague*, 1978 Duke L.J. 1295, 1297 (1978) (ascribing this argument to Charles Black.)

39. Michael Stokes Paulsen, *How to Count to Thirty-Four: The Constitutional Case for a Constitutional Convention*, 34 Harvard Journal of Law and Public Policy 837, 844 (2011).

40. Van Sickle and Boughey, *supra*, at p. 41.

41. *United States v. Sprague*, supra, at pp. 732-733.

42. Letter from James Madison to Thomas Mann Randolph, 13 January 1789, http://founders.archives.gov/documents/Madison/01-11-02-0304, from *Va. Independent Chronicle*, 28 Jan. 1789 (emphasis added.) The

letter from Madison to Randolph refers to the Article V Convention as a General Convention twice, as the next two sentences of the passage confirm again that the duty to call the convention give Congress no power over the convention: "It will not have escaped you, however, that the question concerning a **General Convention** does not depend on the discretion of Congress. If two thirds of the States make application, Congress cannot refuse to call one; if not, Congress have [sic] no right to take the step." (Emphasis added.)

43. Veit, supra, at pp. 6, 96-97, 102-103.

44. Black, supra, at p. 202.

45. U.S. Const., Article IV, Section 4.

46. *Duncan v. McCall*, 139 U.S. 449, 461 (1891) ["By the constitution, **a republican form of government is guaranteed** to every state in the Union, **and the distinguishing feature of that form is the right of the people to choose their own officers for governmental administration** . . ." (Emphasis added.)]

47. 2 Farrand, supra, at p. 665.

48. The Federalist No. 39, at p. 230 (J. Madison) (G. Wills ed. 1982).

49. The Federalist No. 49, at pp. 306-307 (J. Madison) (G. Wills ed. 1982). See also remarks of Colonel Mason on July 23, 1787, 2 Farrand, supra, at p. 88.

50. U.S. Const., Article VII; Thomas H. Neale, *The Article V Convention to Propose Constitutional Amendments: Contemporary Issues for Congress*, Congressional Research Service, at p. 33, April 4, 2014.

51. 51.51. Neale, supra, at p. 33.

52. *Ibid.*, citing Philip L. Martin, "Convention Ratification of Federal Constitutional Amendments," *Political Science Quarterly*, volume LXXXII, no. 1, March, 1967, pp. 61-71.

53. U.S. Const., Amendment Fourteen, Section 1, in part (emphasis added.)

54. John J. Cound, et. al., eds., *Civil Procedure, Cases and Materials*, at p. 209, West Publishing Co., St. Paul, Minn., 1989.

55. *Marshall v. Jerrico, Inc.*, 446 U.S. 238, 242 (1980).

56. *Reynolds v. Sims* 377 U.S. 533, 564-565 (1964).

57. ABA Special Constitutional Convention Study Committee, *Amendment of the Constitution by the Convention Method under Article V*, at p. 33 (1974).

58. *Reynolds v. Sims*, 377 U.S. 533 (1964); *Lucas v. Forty-Fourth General Assembly*, 377 U.S. 713 (1964); *Wesberry v. Sanders*, 376 U.S. 1 (1964)); *Gray v. Sanders*, 372 U.S. 368 (1963).

59. Paul G. Kauper, *The Alternative Amendment Process: Some Observations*, 66 Michigan Law Review 903, 908-909 (1968).

60. Max Farrand, *The Framing of the Constitution of the United States*, at p. 213, Yale University Press, New Haven, Connecticut (1913).

61. Note, *Proposed Legislation on the Convention Method of Amending the United States Constitution*, 85 Harvard L. R. 1612, 1625 (1972).

62. *Id.*, at p. 1624.

63. Charles L. Black, Jr., *Amending The Constitution: A Letter to a Congressman*, 82 Yale L. J. 189, 204-205 (1972).

64. *Reynolds v. Sims*, 377 U.S. 533 (1964); *Lucas v. Forty-Fourth General Assembly*, 377 U.S. 713 (1964); *Wesberry v. Sanders*, 376 U.S. 1 (1964).

65. Walter E. Dellinger, *The Recurring Question of the "Limited" Constitutional Convention*, 88 Yale L. J. 1623, 1633 (1979).

66. *Id.*, at p. 1632.

67. *U.S. Term Limits, Inc. v. Thornton*, supra, at pp. 800-802 (1995).

68. Veit, supra, at p. 6.

69. *U.S. Term Limits, Inc. v. Thornton*, at p. 1633.

70. Neale, supra, at p. 15.

71. *Ibid.*

72. *Leser v. Garnett*, 258 U.S. 130 (1922).

73. *Id.*, at p. 137, citing to *Hawke v. Smith, No. 1*, 253 U.S. 221 (1920) and other cases.

74. See also *U.S. Term Limits, Inc. v. Thornton*, supra, at pp. 782-845, holding that states could not impose term limits on U.S. Congresspersons as the states have no power to change qualifications for Congress that are already set forth in the Constitution.

75. U.S. Const., Article VI, paragraph 3.

76. U.S. Const., Article I, Section 6, paragraph 2.

77. *Coleman v. Miller*, 307 U.S. 433 (1939).

78. *Baker v. Carr*, 369 U.S. 186 (1962).

79. *Id.*, at p. 217.

80. *Ibid.*

81. Paulsen, *A General Theory of Article V: The Constitutional Lessons of the Twenty-Seventh Amendment*, supra, at p. 713.

82. *Baker v. Carr*, supra, at p. 217.

83. *Ibid.*

84. *Ibid.*

85. *Ibid.*

86. Black, supra, at pp. 210-213; Note, *Proposed Legislation on the Convention Method of Amending the United States Constitution*, supra, at pp. 1634-1648; Paulsen, *A General Theory of Article V: The Constitutional Lessons of the Twenty-Seventh Amendment*, supra, at p. 706-721.

87. Rogers, supra, at pp. 1011-1014.

88. Neale, supra, at p. 15, citing Council of State Governments, *The Book of the States*, 2010 edition, volume 42 (Lexington, KY: 2010), p. 13. [The author believes the page citation to The Book of the States is incorrect. The correct pages appear to be pp. 16-17, also denominated as Table 1.4.] States without any rules or procedures set up include

Arkansas, Indiana, Massachusetts, Mississippi, New Jersey, North Dakota, Pennsylvania, and Texas.

89. Paulsen, *How to Count to Thirty-Four: The Constitutional Case for a Constitutional Convention*, supra at p. 847; Van Sickle and Boughey, supra at pp. 63-65.

CHAPTER 10

1. 2 Max Farrand (ed.), *The Records of the Federal Convention of 1787*, at p. 250, Yale University Press, New Haven, Connecticut (1911)

APPENDIX 1

1. Helen E. Veit; Kenneth R. Bowling; Charlene Bangs Bickford (eds.), Creating The Bill of Rights, at pp. 9, 37-41, The Johns Hopkins University Press, Baltimore, Maryland (1991).

2. Id., at pp. 10, 45-49.

3. Id., at pp. 3-4, 11, 49- 50.

4. The originally proposed second amendment is now our Twenty-Seventh Amendment, literally ratified 202 years after its proposal in 1789. See Chapter 2 and http://www.archives.gov/exhibits/charters/ constitution_amendments_11-27.html; http://www.archives.gov/ exhibits/charters/bill_of_rights.html; http://www.archives.gov/exhib-its/charters/bill_of_rights_transcript.html.

5. U.S.C.A., Constitution, Complete Text, at p. 22; http://www.archives. gov/exhibits/charters/bill_of_rights_transcript.html.

ACKNOWLEDGEMENTS

FIRST, I ACKNOWLEDGE AND THANK Fresno attorney Robert Cervantes, for his assistance in proofreading as well as listening for countless hours to my ideas for reforming government. I acknowledge and thank Dr. Robert K. Mitchell, Jr. and Mr. Phillip Cervantes for their continuous encouragement and support. I acknowledge and thank Professor Richard P. Bernstein for his willingness to engage and his insightful criticisms. I acknowledge and thank Lynn M. Boughey for his communication and feedback. Finally, I acknowledge all teachers, professors and mentors who encourage us to achieve beyond our training and education.

BIBLIOGRAPHY

"75% in U.S. See Widespread Government Corruption," Gallup (September 19, 2015), http://www.gallup.com/poll/185759/widespread-government-corruption.aspx.

ABA Special Constitutional Convention Study Committee, *Amendment of the Constitution by the Convention Method under Article V* (1974).

Akhil Reed Amar, *The Bill of Rights as a Constitution*, 100 Yale L. J. 1131 (1991).

Americans' Views on Money in Politics, New York Times (June 2, 2015), http://nyti.ms/1KAz5AE.

Richard P. Bernstein, *The Sleeper Wakes: The History and Legacy of the Twenty-Seventh Amendment*, 61 Fordham L. Rev. 497 (1992).

Charles L. Black, Jr., *Amending The Constitution: A Letter to a Congressman*, 82 Yale L. J. 189 (1972).

Arthur Earl Bonfield, *The Dirksen Amendment and the Article V Convention Process*, 66 Mich. L. R. 949 (1968).

Ida A. Brudnick, *Salaries of Members of Congress: Recent Actions and Historical Tables*, Congressional Research Service, December 19, 2014.

Richard L. Burke, The Los Angeles Times, *1789 Amendment is Ratified But Now the Debate Begins*, May 8, 1992.

Ben Casselman, *"The Slow Death of American Entrepreneurship,"* FiveThirtyEight (May 15, 2014), http://fivethirtyeight.com/features/the-slow-death-of-american-entrepreneurship/.

"Congressional Research Belongs to the Public," The New York Times (June 17, 2015), http://nyti.ms/1MKeJp6.

John J. Cound, et. al., eds., *Civil Procedure, Cases and Materials*, West Publishing Co., St. Paul, Minn., 1989.

Walter E. Dellinger, *The Recurring Question of the "Limited" Constitutional Convention*, 88 Yale L. J. 1623 (1979).

Everett McKinley Dirksen, *The Supreme Court and The People*, 66 Michigan L. Rev. 837 (1968).

3 *Debates on The Adoption of the Federal Constitution*, Washington, D.C. (J. Elliot ed. 1836) ["ELLIOT'S DEBATES"].

Sam J. Ervin, Jr., *Proposed Legislation to Implement the Convention Method of Amending the Constitution*, 66 Michigan L. Rev. 875 (1968).

Max Farrand, *The Framing of the Constitution of the United States*, Yale University Press, New Haven, Connecticut (1913).

1 Max Farrand (ed.), *The Records of the Federal Convention of 1787*, Yale University Press, New Haven, Connecticut (1911).

2 Max Farrand (ed.), *The Records of the Federal Convention of 1787*, Yale University Press, New Haven, Connecticut (1911).

3 Max Farrand (ed.), *The Records of the Federal Convention of 1787*, Yale University Press, New Haven, Connecticut (1911)., Yale University Press, New Haven, Connecticut (1911).

The Federalist Papers (A. Hamilton, J. Madison, J. Jay), Bantam Dell, New York, N.Y. (G. Wills ed. 1982).

George Washington's Farewell Address, Senate Document No. 106–21, Washington, D.C. (2000)

George Washington's Inaugural Address, April 30, 1789, http://www.archives.gov/exhibits/american_originals/inaugtxt.html

Glendon, Gordon & Osakwe, *Comparative Legal Traditions*, West Publishing Co., St. Paul, Minn. (1985).

Glendon, Gordon & Osakwe, *Comparative Legal Traditions in a Nutshell*, West Publishing Co., St. Paul, Minn. (1982).

Jeffrey M. Jones, *Democratic, Republican Identification Near Historical Lows*, Gallup, January 11, 2016, http://www.gallup.com/poll/188096/democratic-republican-identification-near-historical-lows.aspx.

Jeffrey M. Jones, "*Trust in Federal Government on Domestic Matters Edges to New Low*," Gallup (September 24, 2015), http://www.gallup.com/poll/185876/trust-federal-gov-domestic-matters-edges-new-low.aspx.

Paul G. Kauper, *The Alternative Amendment Process: Some Observations*, 66 Michigan L. Rev. 903 (1968).

David M. Kennedy, *Freedom From Fear: The American People in Depression and War, 1929-1945*, Oxford University Press, New York, N.Y. (1999).

Kurt T. Lash, *The Lost Original Meaning of the Ninth Amendment*, 83 Texas L. Rev. 331 (December 2004).

David S. Law; Mila Versteeg, *The Declining Influence of the United States Constitution*, 87 N.Y.U. L. R. 762 (2012).

Los Angeles Times, *Los Angeles Riots: 20 Years Later*, April 28, 2014, http://www.latimes.com/la-me-los-angeles-riots-sg-storygallery.html.

Donald S. Lutz, *Popular Consent and Popular Control*, Louisiana State University Press, Baton Rouge, Louisiana (1980).

Philip L. Martin, "Convention Ratification of Federal Constitutional Amendments," *Political Science Quarterly*, volume LXXXII, no. 1, March, 1967.

Justin McCarthy, *"No Improvement in Congress Approval, at 13%,"* Gallup (March 9, 2016), http://www.gallup.com/poll/189848/no-improvement-congress-approval.aspx.

Thomas H. Neale, *The Article V Convention to Propose Constitutional Amendments: Contemporary Issues for Congress*, Congressional Research Service, July 9, 2012.

Thomas H. Neale, *The Article V Convention to Propose Constitutional Amendments: Contemporary Issues for Congress*, Congressional Research Service, April 4, 2014.

Thomas H. Neale, *The Article V Convention to Propose Constitutional Amendments: Contemporary Issues for Congress*, Congressional Research Service, March 29, 2016.

Thomas H. Neale, *The Article V Convention to Propose Constitutional Amendments: Current Developments*, Congressional Research Service, March 29, 2016.

Thomas H. Neale, *The Article V Convention for Proposing Constitutional Amendments: Historical Perspectives for Congress*, Congressional Research Service, October 22, 2012.

Frank Newport, *"Half in U.S. Continue to Say Government is an Immediate Threat,"* Gallup (September 21, 2015), http://www.gallup.com/poll/185720/half-continue-say-gov-immediate-threat.aspx.

Jim Norman, *"Public Remains Wary of Federal Government's Power,"* Gallup (October 9, 2015), http://www.gallup.com/poll/186065/public-remains-wary-federal-government-power.aspx.

Note, *Proposed Legislation on the Convention Method of Amending the United States Constitution*, 85 Harvard L. R. 1612 (1972).

Michael Stokes Paulsen, *A General Theory of Article V: The Constitutional Lessons of the Twenty-Seventh Amendment*, 103 Yale L. J. 677 (1993).

Michael Stokes Paulsen, *How to Count to Thirty-Four: The Constitutional Case for a Constitutional Convention*, 34 Harvard Journal of Law & Public Policy 837 (2011).

Pew Research Center, November, 2015, *"Beyond Distrust: How Americans View Their Government "*

Restatement of the Law (Second) Contracts, American Law Institute Publishers, St. Paul, MN (1981).

James Kenneth Rogers, *The Other Way to Amend the Constitution: The Article V Constitutional Convention Amendment Process*, 30 Harvard J. of L. & P. P. 1005 (2007).

Sabrina Tavarnise, *"Disparity in Life Spans of the Rich and the Poor is Growing,"* The New York Times (February 12, 2016), http://nyti.ms/1RwgE6h.

Lawrence H. Tribe, *American Constitutional Law*, The Foundation Press, Inc., Mineola, New York (1988).

William W. Van Alstyne, *Does Article V Restrict the States to Calling Unlimited Conventions Only? – A Letter to a Colleague*, 1978 Duke L.J. 1295, 1297 (1978).

Bruce M. Van Sickle; Lynn M. Boughey, *A Lawful and Peaceful Revolution: Article V and Congress' Present Duty to Call a Convention For Proposing Amendments*, 14 Hamline L. Rev. 1 (1990).

Helen E. Veit; Kenneth R. Bowling; Charlene Bangs Bickford (eds.), *Creating The Bill of Rights: The Documentary Record from the First Federal Congress*, The Johns Hopkins University Press, Baltimore, Maryland (1991).

United States Code Annotated, Constitution, Thompson West (2004).

Gordon S. Wood, *The Creation of the American Republic 1776-1789*, The University of North Carolina Press, Chapel Hill, North Carolina (1969).

CASE LAW

Baker v. Carr, 369 U.S. 186 (1962).

Citizens United v. Federal Election Commission, 558 U.S. 310 (2010).

Coleman v. Miller, 307 U.S. 433 (1939).

Cook v. Gralike, 531 U.S. 510 (2001).

District of Columbia v. Heller, 554 U.S. 570 (2008).

Gray v. Sanders, 372 U.S. 368 (1963).

Korematsu v. United States, 323 U.S. 214 (1944).

Leser v. Garnett, 258 U.S. 130 (1922).

Lucas v. Forty-Fourth General Assembly, 377 U.S. 713 (1964)

Morehead v. New York ex rel. Tipaldo, 298 U.S. 587 (1936).

M'Culloch v. Maryland, 17 U.S. 316 (1819).

Reynolds v. Sims, 377 U.S. 533 (1964).

U.S. Term Limits, Inc. v. Thornton, 514 U.S. 779 (1995).

United States v. Sprague, 282 U.S. 716 (1931).

Wesberry v. Sanders, 376 U.S. 1 (1964).

West Coast Hotel v. Parrish[1], 300 U.S. 379 (1937).

Wickard v. Filburn, 317 U.S. 111 (1942).